I have called you by your name; you are mine.
(Isaiah, Ch. 43, v. 1)

GRANDAD, YOU'RE NOT PAINTING BETWEEN THE LINES

A MEMOIR OF SORTS

Frank Marshall

With every good wish & appreciation

Frank Marshall

ISBN-13: 978-1500451622
ISBN-10: 1500451622

www.frankmarshall.ie

This first paperback edition printed by CreateSpace.

Cover design and interior layout by Averill Buchanan.

The cover shows the author cycling into the River Suir fully clothed for a bet of ten shillings in 1955.

For my family: Maree, Kevin, David and Niamh

The following, who are no longer with us, are specially remembered: Kevin Pyke, Paddy Darcy, Jimmy O'Halloran, Frank Fraser, Mick Lynch.

Also Johnnie Hughes, Kevin O'Brien, Colm O'Doherty, Peter Nugent, Sean Cahill, Fr Jack O'Leary SJ, Fr Columban Heaney OCSO and Maurice Twoomey, to all of whom I owe a special gratitude.

Acknowledgements

I thank: my editor, Brendan O'Brien, for his efficiency, dedication and infinite patience, all of which got us over the line; Stephen Kelly for his unfailing support; Mary Butler, Arts Officer and Niamh Finn, Kilkenny Arts Office; RTÉ Radio 1 and Lyric fm, which broadcast the original versions of twenty-one chapters, and the producers, Martha McCarron, Liz Sweeney and Jacqui Corcoran; Maire Nic Ghearailt and Eoin Brady, producers and editors of the *The Quiet Quarter* and *The Anthologies*; Mary Craddock and Gerry Cody, director and producer, Watergate Productions, and the cast of the Radio Kilkenny production of *A River Walk*; Monica Furlong, director and cast of Shoestring Radio Theatre, San Francisco, for the revised version, and RTÉ Producer Scott Fredericks and the Coolmine Drama Circle cast for the RTÉ Production; Joe Kenny, photographer and editor of the *Fethard and Killusty Review* for the photograph of 'The Gladiator'; Paddy Lonergan for the Padraic Fallon correspondence in Wexford C&E; Tom Jordan OP, editor of *Spirituality*; Trevor White, editor of *The Dubliner* magazine; Pat Murphy, editor of *Stroan Literary Review*; Gerard Moloney CSsR, editor of *Reality* magazine; Seamus Mac Gabhan, editor of *The Customs Journal*; Ciaran Pringle, editor and Martina West of *RevInniu*; Tom Corr, editor and Eamonn Wynne of the *Clonmel Nationalist*, who published two chapters in 2008; and Emer Foley, presenter of the *Arts Show* on KCLR Radio with Gobnait Kearney for providing the privilege and undeniable challenge of live radio reviewing over five years.

Patrons

Johnie Hughes and Eamonn Langton.

Contents

INTRODUCTION

I can remember the exact moment when the magic words were uttered. At the kitchen table Heather and I were beavering away at our respective colouring books. While never the most distinguished performer, I was quietly pleased with my efforts.

'Granddad, you're not painting between the lines.'

This was a serious admonishment – nothing frivolous in the tone. It was not surprising, as Heather often cautioned me. My reaction never varied; I always seemed to look for more tolerance with some humour, but often met no more than a deep sigh of exasperation not uncommon in some four-year-olds. Heather was always engaging and challenging but also lovable. The moment passed without any real resolution.

It was some time later that I began to think again about the phrase. It stayed with me, and it is easy in hindsight to make too much out of it. However, on a very simple level it seemed to me that I had lived a great deal of my life without taking too much notice of these so-called 'lines'. I took early retirement in 1996; three years later on the occasion of a funeral of a former colleague, another colleague shook my hand and, with a suitable accompanying grin, asked: 'Why is it that when nearly everyone had long hair you had very short hair, and now when almost everyone has very short hair you have very long hair?'

My answer was spontaneous without being too profound: 'Maybe that's because of the way I am, and then maybe not?'

More laughter, but I realised that while this man had known me over ten years in the same official location, it may have been no more than a bit of harmless 'slagging'. It also struck me that there may have been a deeper implication. It would not have been the first time that it was suggested that I was in the wrong job. When I started to think about this book I was convinced that the title was ideal irrespective of how I was seen, and I don't

1

feel that it is necessary to justify its use. Who knows what will emerge for the reader? Time will tell … hopefully?

I had broadcast a total of twenty-seven short pieces over a number of years on RTÉ Radio 1 and Lyric fm, on *The Quiet Quarter*, *Sunday Miscellany* and *The Living Word*; I began writing additional material of recollection and finally found it hard to stop. Maybe I needed another imperious rejoinder from a young mind. I am grateful to very many people for their help and encouragement and have listed some of them, but mere words are often just not adequate.

1

SEARCHING

'I always knew you were a bloody chancer, Frankie – now I know the reason.'

Before I could respond to this unusual greeting on the telephone the caller continued, clearly enjoying himself.

'Why does your great grandmother appear as 47 in the 1901 census and miraculously ageing to 73 in the 1911 one?'

The caller – another Frank, and a former colleague – had encouraged me to trace my ancestry, offering to start the process. I gave him the names of my great grandparents and very quickly he responded that in the 1901 census he had found – to use his own phrase – 'three Catholic women residing in a lane off Patrick Street in Kilkenny city'. It seemed that he had discovered Bridget Marshall, my great grandmother, and two of her daughters, Margaret and Alice.

He needed no encouragement to look at the 1911 census, and provided the answer to his unusual opening comment. Old age pensions had been introduced in 1908. Bridget Marshall was clearly a very resourceful woman. There is little doubt that she would not have hesitated to make a few extra shillings by altering her age. This was a lady who had given birth to eleven children, six of whom had survived. Her life would have been one of endless drudgery, struggling to provide for her large family. Domestic service in the houses of the local gentry would have been the only possibility of earning a few shillings.

1901 census form

1911 census form

Remarkably, there was no trace of David Marshall, my great grandfather, on either census form. Was it a simple coincidence that he was absent on both nights? There is the stark fact that both official forms describe Bridget as 'Head of family'. So where was David on the nights in question? It remains a mystery. The absence of my grandfather, Francis, was easily explained by his military service.

I trawled through the local church records in St Patrick's parish, having failed miserably to find anything in the civil ones. On the point of abandoning the search, I was astonished to find that in one week in November 1907, two weddings took place in that family. The third daughter, Bridget, and her brother, Joseph, both married local partners. Bridget Keeffe and David Marshall were listed as the parents in both entries. It was a strange feeling to see David's name, which was borne by my late father and now by my younger son. There was some relief when the name appeared in the cold black ink of officialdom. However, his name on the form did not mean that he was still alive then.

In any case, there were two weddings from one family on different days in the same week, when the average for the period, according to the register, was one wedding every two or three months. I put my imagination on hold again and accepted the records, rejoicing in the discovery of my great grandfather.

Some years later, having almost forgotten about the family history, unexpectedly I managed to access local records in another parish which revealed the marriage of David Marshall from Vicar Street to Bridget Keeffe from Green Street in St Canice's Catholic church in Kilkenny city on 26 September 1870. This was a hugely satisfying discovery – beyond words, almost. The family lived in New Building Lane in the centre of the city before moving eventually to a tiny house in Gooseberry Lane, off Upper Patrick Street.

The really astonishing thing was my own slow realisation that a lady named Annie, my grand-aunt featuring in the 1911 census, was none other than the lady who served us ham and tomatoes in her house in Dominick Street, Kilkenny in July 1950. I had travelled from Clonmel with my father, his two brothers Frankie and Christy and their sister May for the Leinster hurling final between Kilkenny and Wexford. I remember Annie as a small, cheerful lady, excited to see her Tipperary relations. These were her late brother Francis' children and there was much warmth and celebration at the reunion. On the day I was not remotely concerned with my origins. The adults were excited even as Tipperary natives at Kilkenny's triumph.

The clear recollection of this visit to Annie's house transformed my attitude to this entire family. All the anomalies about dates were seen as inconsequential and irrelevant. I began to warm to them as real, recognisable and lovable people who survived in very difficult times in a parish less than a mile from where I now reside. Later I learned from Ned Byrne – famous as the only man to win an All-Ireland hurling medal with Kilkenny and an Irish international rugby cap – that Annie had worked in his family home as a cleaner. 'A great character, a lovely woman, she was one of the last women to wear a shawl in Kilkenny and like yourself, Frank, she smoked a pipe.'

In an earlier version of this piece, which I read on *The Quiet Quarter* on Lyric fm, my vivid imagination had broached the possibility of our family being connected to William Marshall, who built Kilkenny Castle in 1195. This was based on the discovery that Gooseberry Lane was in the environs of the Castle.

Now this was seen as no more than fanciful speculation, and was allowed to drift. Annie might have had an interesting comment on the idea.

2

THE KING'S SHILLING

My grandfather Francis would have found 'the King's shilling' an attractive proposition as a young man. A private's life in the British Army would not have been all joy, but it offered a chance of freedom and adventure a great deal more exciting than the confines of Gooseberry Lane. It is not unreasonable to imagine him dreaming of the day when he could enlist. Very many young men at the time must have longed for the prospect of escaping just anywhere into the great unknown. A garrison town would have produced its own folklore.

Could Francis have foreseen that his discharge papers would show two periods of service in India together with a year in South Africa over twenty-one years up to 1913, and then reenlisting in 1913 and serving a further three years in India? He reenlisted again in 1916, finally retiring in 1919 after twenty-seven years of dedicated service.

Francis enlisted in Kilkenny on 23 March 1892. In his service record is a document which shows that he had an official record of 'Drilling' over a period of three years previously. This signified a clear, premeditated plan to support his chance of enlistment. It is easy to think of the imaginative dreaming that would have preoccupied Francis as he anticipated becoming a soldier.

Private Francis C. Marshall

Two days after his enlistment in Kilkenny, his service record shows his enlistment in Clonmel. This resulted in the eventual emergence of another branch of the Marshall family in Tipperary. An imaginative account of Francis' journey from Kilkenny is contained in my brother Oliver's poem 'The King's Shilling', which was written long before I traced our grandfather's service record. Published in 1986 in *New Irish Writing*, in 2005 it was included in the collection *Father's Day* (Summer Palace Press)

In February 1904 Francis returned to Clonmel, having soldiered for nine years in India and a year in South Africa. He must have been very glad to be back. Over the next few months he succumbed to the charms of Bridget Barret in Clonmel, where they were married in 1906. She was just 17 and my father was born a year later: it is hard to imagine what their life was like in their small house in School House Lane, but unquestionably it was very different to his time abroad.

Early in 1907 Francis came home to his young wife and told her that his regiment had been posted to India again. It was customary that spouses accompanied their husbands overseas and it would be naïve to think that Bridget had much choice in the matter; yet some part of me believes that Francis might have asked Bridget, who was expecting their second child at this stage, if she wished to go with him to India. I can picture the scene as she sat down at the kitchen table holding my father in her arms and trying to cope with this momentous option.

Bridget Marshall

The news may have left her in a state of numbed shock – she had never left Clonmel. The thought of travelling halfway around the world may have terrified her. My grandmother lived until I was a young adult, but we never talked about India. My own Ma once said 'Granny did not like India' – that is the only clue. The families of enlisted men did not travel first class, conditions would have been primitive, and she minded a toddler while pregnant and travelling by boat from Dublin to England and then down through the South Atlantic via the Bay of Biscay, notorious for stormy weather; edging around the Cape of Good Hope and moving up the straits of the Indian Ocean. I can imagine Bridget longing for School House Lane and wondering vainly if this sickening motion would ever cease.

The unrelenting heat coupled with recurring sea sickness, quite apart from the normal travails of pregnancy, would have exhausted her. The fearful nagging inner voice of the young mother would have been hard to shake off, and even Francis' genuine care would hardly have been enough. She was always a great lady for the prayers when I knew her later, and I can picture her fingering her rosary beads along the way as the ship skated and slithered over tumultuous seas in the vicinity of the Cape. Clonmel must have seemed on a different planet.

They spent over five years in India; my uncle Frankie was born there and Bridget also had a miscarriage. The lack of information about their precise location provoked me into considering a trip to India to retrace their journey. A visit to the office of British war records in Kew in 1996 turned into a tiresome trawl through voluminous carded records and computer screens. On seven different occasions my heart missed a beat as I came across the name 'Francis Marshall', all of whom served during the period, but all were English born. As a last resort I turned to a professional researcher, but even her diligent efforts proved fruitless. My sense of disappointment must have conveyed itself to my uncle Paddy, as out of the blue he produced a sheaf of documents from the family archives. A regimental bulletin of the Royal Irish Regiment dated 13 February 1913 contained the following paragraph:

> Naizriabad Saturday 15th February 1913, to pension no. 4371 Private F. Marshall D Company accompanied by his wife and two children, this family will be dispatched direct from Kigali to port of embarkation.

The cold black ink of officialdom was sufficient under the hand of Major E.F. Milner Commanding 1st Battalion Royal Irish Regiment. It authenticated all my father's stories and gave them a sense of place. There was no need to head off in search of their footsteps.

Passing Out Parade
(in memory of Francis C. Marshall)

Army band playing softly, flapping tents
half sheltering the privileged groups.
Gentle mist touching the assembled outsiders,
as departing troops march proudly by.

United Nations Battalion destined for Lebanon
solemn faced men and women sadly almost
indistinguishable in the dull formless khaki.

Young women with buggies
Lifting infants in a forlorn hope of
showing fathers or even mothers.

How many turned out for your day
in 1892? Did Queen Victoria send
her envoy? Or did the *Kilkenny People*
in its first year cover your safari?

India, Burma, South Africa via Clonmel
twenty-one years a Royal Irish Fusilier.
Proudly, I imagine you searching for
your beloved mother in her best shawl.

3

A MAN OF MANY PARTS

Usually around tea time on Saturdays in the late 1940s the local insurance man arrived in our house. It was Bill's last call of the day and he was never in a hurry to leave. His breezy good humour was infectious and it enlivened the household, particularly my grandfather as he reposed in the kitchen armchair.

Almost unfailingly in the midst of the recounting of the local news – and Bill would have visited innumerable houses – the story of 'the car' would emerge: 'God, Paddy it would be a good night to have your big shiny car instead of my auld crock of a bike.'

Over fifty years later I can remember the softening smile as my grandfather listened quietly to the dramatic tale of the Gladiator's huge silver-coloured steel frame trundling down the Fethard road into Clonmel. Unquestionably there would have been great interest in this invention, but Bill suggested that nearly half the population of Clonmel were on the Railway Bridge in a frenzy of excitement.

'It must have been a great feeling at the wheel of that huge big yoke? Where did ya learn to drive anyway? Sure ya were one of the most famous men around then, and to think it was the first registered car in South Tipperary in 1903. HI 1, a part of history.'

Grandfather rarely added anything except to clarify that he was the driver and not the owner. This was during his sojourn as house steward with the Burke family in Grove House, Fethard. It was very clear that he enjoyed the fuss and the attention. It was the highlight of his week. I was entranced by this weekly performance in the kitchen, but there was a note of poignancy when my mother told me many years later that the parting handshake between the two men covered the surreptitious passing of a half crown to my grandfather.

'The Gladiator', first registered car in South Tipperary, with Paddy Kenrick (driver, at front) and William Burke (owner) in 1906

This generous gesture facilitated an occasional foray in his wheelchair to the local pub. This depended on a 'driver' and normally they were reliable, but sadly one neglected to collect him at closing time. There was no sober volunteer in the pub to negotiate the few hundred yards to his home. Like many such stories it developed legs over the years, but it seems a new brand of colourful language was heard on the night.

Patrick Kenrick, the eldest of fourteen children, was born in 1872 and grew up in Fethard, Co. Tipperary. He had an extraordinarily varied life and worked as a tailor, a house steward, a clerk in the Army, a school attendance officer and a small shopkeeper. The job of house steward was an onerous one. He was responsible for paying wages to the staff, many of whom lived on the premises. As the main chauffeur to the Burke family he was constantly on the move, and on one occasion drove from Holyhead to London in the beloved Gladiator. One very interesting event that arose out of his position as steward was the birth of my mother in Grove House. He was able to arrange this, and it always gave her great satisfaction to talk about it over the years.

It is difficult to grasp the range of occupations held by Paddy Kenrick, but apparently he was a remarkably enterprising spirit who grasped any opportunity that arose. The Ma told me that he went to Tralee, Co. Kerry as a consultant on the installation of electricity there. It appears that Fethard had been endowed with the new invention and the bold Paddy managed to sell his experience to the Kerry folk. There is an absence of hard information on this saga, and I often wondered just how it all happened.

Paddy's wife Mary Ellen (née Phelan) may well have been overshadowed by this multi-talented man, but she was actively involved in the Singer sewing shop in O'Connell Street in Clonmel, which both of them ran for a period in the early 1930s. Their daughter Peggy (the Ma) often told me that she loved the time they spent there, as she was actively involved in the venture as a young woman.

There is the old cliché about the strong woman supporting the active public man, and it may have been a lot more than supposition in this case. The Kenricks rented a house at 2 Queen Street in the 1930s, but it was highly unorthodox in that they paid the previous tenant a sum of money to become key holders without the landlord's permission. The case ended up in court but the verdict went in their favour, and it became the family home from then on. Sadly Mary Ellen died in 1937 at the relatively young age of 53.

Another of Paddy Kenrick's talents came to light many years after his death when a large number of photographic glass-plated negatives were unearthed by Tony Newport, Paddy's nephew – after insistent prodding by my mother – hidden in a disused room in the old family home in Fethard. These were handed over to another Kenrick descendant, Joe Kenny, a professional photographer in Fethard. He did a magnificent job of processing and developing them, revealing a very interesting and unusual collection of photographs. Experts have acknowledged them as a remarkable reflection of the social spectrum of the early twentieth century. They include the local gentry, the Royal Irish Constabulary and the plain people of South Tipperary. The National Museum and local museums in Fethard and Clonmel now hold copies under the title of 'The Kenrick Collection'. Not surprisingly, Paddy's son Joe inherited the photographic skills, producing a prodigious number of photographs in the UK, where he resided with his family.

Confined to a wheelchair towards the end of his days, Paddy occasionally sat outside the house in Clonmel and chatted with locals. Apparently he rarely, if ever, referred to his former exploits. I was too young then to have engaged him in any kind of meaningful dialogue. As a young adult I had a recurring nightmare for a period in which I was told the complete story of his life but forgot it all because of my lack of attention.

The publication of the poem 'The Gladiator', which celebrated part of my grandfather's achievements, at least made some recompense for the earlier neglect, as did the reading of part of this chapter on Lyric fm.

Patrick Kenrick died in 1950, aged 78. One week later I was given his bedroom, and I still remember that first night – it was a Thursday – as I lay fearfully in the bed in which he had spent his last night. It was eerie, even though I had asked that the light be left on. I slept peacefully, no doubt watched over by his benign spirit.

The Gladiator
(in memory of Patrick Kenrick)

Framed in an eight inch photograph
The majesty of the Gladiator somewhat dimmed.
What was it like in 1904 to drive
The first registered motor car in South Tipperary?

Your only unfailing weekly visitor
Enlivened your boredom.
We all came running as we heard it
Coming over the first bridge in Clonmel.

Those later years were cruel
Far removed from the mighty Gladiator.
Poor circulation, the curse of the elderly
In the fifties, caused the loss of a leg.

Things could have been better ordered
Between us, you spent so much time telling me
To be quiet, rather than regaling me with tales of wonder.
We spent our time competing for another's affection.

Forgotten in the pub by the local clown
You would have pined for the Gladiator,
As you sat in sadness in your wheelchair
with barely enough drink to oil your wheels.

4

THE BANKER

The front window of our house looked out on two small adjoining houses straight across the street. In one of those John lived alone. He had been rechristened 'the Banker' by the locals.

The Banker's career began in earnest in the spring of 1953, when Baron's Park won the Lincoln at odds of 33/1. His one pound each way bet netted him forty-two pounds. The word spread rapidly among the younger gang in the locality. There were only thirteen houses in our row, with no gardens front or back. The phrase 'three up, two down' neatly defined them. We were a closely knit community, and this win was seen as a fortune – more than a month's wage for any of the residents.

This spectacular coup was followed up with a long run of even greater success. These events are always prone to exaggeration, but the Banker began hiring a hackney car twice a week to take him to the greyhound tracks in two nearby towns, and it was very clear that it was not all being run on 'lucky bag' money. It seemed he could not pick a loser. None of the local bookmakers were glad to see him arriving, as it was evident that he was on a roll and very few people gambled so wildly then and with such abandon.

The nature of the street meant that it was impossible to keep any secrets. The Banker was often the topic of the day, every day. His parents had died and the rest of the family had taken the emigrant boat. He was likely to be seen swinging from the signpost adjacent to his house, or sitting on the window ledge studying form. The Banker was only about twenty then, and there was general goodwill for him on the street. Packie – unemployed, dreadfully short of money, and not in great physical shape – would have been the exception.

'Imagine I saw that clown up there standing over a manhole cover in the middle of the road, trying to drop single shillings through the small slit, throwing money down the shore – never in all my life!'

His voice trembled as he asked for five Woodbines in the local shop, and the look of desolation at the waste he had witnessed was pitiable.

There were many hilarious moments. Once, rather than buy an alarm clock, the Banker tied a piece of twine around his big toe and hung the twine out the top window. Pulling the twine earned me the sum of two shillings. The Ma was less than impressed by this, wondering what I would do with the money.

The Banker was very generous with a few of us who were still at school. He would stand us the price of the matinée at the local cinema very often. Once when he had not responded to our overtures he opened the top window and flung a fistful of change at us to get rid of us. This was uncharacteristic. He believed in spending, and the bigger the splash the better. He dressed extremely well on his trips to the greyhound tracks. A Crombie coat, yellow knitted gloves to match and a silk scarf – at twenty this style was making more than the locals take notice. The Banker had two close friends who went everywhere with him. Extremely loyal, Michael and Fergie hung on his every word, sometimes placing the bets for him as he stood smoking in all his glory in the stand at the dog track. It was like a scene from a Jimmy Cagney film.

Occasionally a few of us managed to climb over the wall and get into the race track. The Banker was not happy with our presence, which clearly was inspired by his own celebrity. He actually warned us and told us to clear off home a few times. Often there was a pay-off when he relented after a successful night; we were allowed back into the circle and treated to lemonade and rock buns, which was far preferable to studying Latin or Irish grammar. On the way home one night three of us, suitably stuffed with rock buns and fizzy lemonade and full of the excitement of the night's racing, were confronted by my father.

Clearly very angry, he roared at me and ordered me home. This was the first time I had seen him – normally a very quiet, mild-mannered man – in such an agitated state. It was clear that I was in serious trouble – even my two friends were bothered. I was home in a flash. My Dad lectured me on the evils of gambling: he was fearful that I was being lured down the slippery slope. I can't recall if there was any serious curtailment of my lifestyle, but his uncharacteristic reaction left its mark.

All of this good fortune and its display never attracted any young women into the Banker's circle. That never occurred to me at the time, but looking back it seemed just a little curious that there were no obvious girlfriends around. However, the gambling would probably have been a deterrent in itself, and the ever-vigilant mothers would have been appalled and very wary of a so-called gambler associating with their daughters. Anyway, the two henchmen Michael and Fergie, who were single-minded in their dedication to his protection, would have tolerated no deflection towards such trivial pursuits as chasing young wans.

Sometimes on Sundays the Banker hired a hackney and took a few of us to the seaside; on one particular outing there was great excitement as we scoffed a huge meal in a hotel. It was the first time in such an establishment for most of us. Three or four of us would not have a shilling between us, and we just couldn't believe our luck. We were safe as houses with him, and I think even then I could see a certain naïveté in him, but without the ability to put the words on my feelings.

It is hard to be sure just how long it all lasted; not more than two years. It was rumoured on and off that he was not doing too well. We knew that there had to be some losses, but I thought it would go on forever. Of course there were some that were wildly jealous and were almost waiting for his downfall.

The end came quickly. In spite of the rumours, no one could believe it when he left. It was said he had to borrow the fare to go to England. There was genuine sadness in the street. I can still remember the shock I felt when I heard he had left. He avoided any ceremony. One morning the revelation was made: 'The Banker is left – gone to Blighty.'

I was devastated. He was a good-natured guy who brought genuine excitement into my life, and a fair few shillings as well.

He came home on holidays once. I had left home at that stage. The Ma said he had changed a lot. That was it. He never came back. Various reports of people claiming to have met him circulated back to the street. He left his mark, but in time it faded. He has long since passed on to the race meetings in the sky.

5

EXODUS

On a rain lashed Monday in the fifties
five sad faced brothers lost and lonely
swept away in the 7.30 to Rosslare.
Only specks in the weekly throng
herded on crowded crafts in the Irish Sea.
Deep anxiety among our tiny group about
the half saved youngest 'Skippy' who
flapped around the town, unschooled but not
untamed, poor material for the wilds of Kilburn.
One suitcase wrapped with twine a bundle
of near rags encircled in their hopes.
Their leaving developed into legend all
magnified with porter. The sad cold story of
their non-return is almost unremembered now.

A half-hearted attempt to leave 'Skippy' at home failed. He was seen as 'not quite right' in the language of the time; the other brothers hoped that one of the families where he spent most of his time would look after him. Word got out in the tightly knit community, and the mothers told the eldest brother that they would not be allowed to leave without 'Skippy'.

He had never gone to school for very long, and Skippy didn't emerge from his home until he was almost six. After a month's exposure in the locality he was withdrawn by his protective and partially disabled mother. He languished at home again until he was near nine. All of this occurred in spite of the rigours of the school attendance officer, commonly known as the 'Cruelty Man'. When Skippy finally emerged to roam at will, he became 'street wise' very quickly, but in Paddies Land he would have been at serious risk.

Skippy had a large mop of fairish hair which had never seen the inside of a barber's shop. Coupled with his long black overcoat, which had seen better days, he was a striking figure. A very loud voice, which at times could sound like a foghorn, was enhanced by the odd four-letter word. If you were in the company of Skippy he kept you alert, if only because of his constant movement. He just never stood still. In reality he was as meek as a doll.

He followed Anne everywhere like a lap dog. We shared an interest in Anne, who was six months older than me. My interest was more specific, as I was more than a little attracted to her, but there was not a hint of it being reciprocated. She gave me the same old 'Howya' and that was it, no matter where or when we met. Skippy's penetrating stare was always a reminder that my interest in Anne might be misplaced.

Anne didn't appear on the night of the departure, and it was very sad to see Skippy gazing out the back window of the bus. The anxious faces of the travellers were mirrored in our expressions of loss and concern.

I never laid an eye on them after that fateful night. They came back once or twice, but I had long left home. Many stories were told about their exploits, some of which were suitably adorned and exaggerated. However, it seems that Skippy got lost in the early days in the wilds of London town and was rescued by the police. There was an inevitability about it all.

When they were very young, I regularly regaled my two sons at bedtime with various versions of the whole saga. Eventually one said: 'I'm tired of that story about Skippy – tell us another story, Daddy.'

Neither Kevin nor David has claimed ownership of the statement.

Clonmel High School Drama, winners at Clonmel and Dundrum Feiseanna 1955 (back B. O'Mahony, Michael Burke, the author, Dermot Moloughney; front Martin Carey, T.J. Meagher (Director), Tony O'Brien)

6

CYCLING FOR INSPIRATION

It's amazing how often we look back into the past and speculate about how easily our lives could have turned out differently. Some of us even think occasionally what it would have been like if we had opted for a different partner. Listening to a friend speculating about this recently, I was reminded that my mother told me many years ago that when my father asked her to marry him, she didn't agree immediately. Instead she looked for time to consider the proposal: her exact wording is unclear, but what is undisputed is that she took herself off to Mount Melleray Abbey on her bicycle and spent a few days in contemplation.

Cycling the twenty miles from her home in Clonmel on an old Raleigh bike must have been a lonely journey for a 24-year-old in 1937. I was astonished when she told me this story. It seemed a most unusual reaction even for such an independent woman. Now, with hindsight, I see it as a very prudent decision. She became very vague about the decision process when I questioned her. 'Ah I did a bit of praying and talked to one of the monks.' It was left at that. The Ma duly returned on her bike having made up her mind: it must have been an exhilarating spin down the Knockmealdown Mountains.

She accepted my father's proposal, and they were married in February 1938. I never ventured to ask my father about his reaction to her initial response. I feel he might have been too shy to discuss it, or maybe it was my own shyness. Their contentment over forty-eight years together was quite obvious, and I never saw any evidence of regret about her decision, yet I often wondered over the years about what would have happened if that pairing had not taken place.

Recently all the speculation was resurrected as I cycled up that same road from Clonmel to Mount Melleray: it's a steep, unrelenting climb from Newcastle to the monastery. I couldn't escape the thought of the Ma pushing her old bike up those fierce hills in search of inspiration.

Over the years she continued to go back, usually driven by my father in his prized Morris Minor. In 1997, a few months before she died, I took her up to the monastery; as usual she seemed peaceful leaving. Over the years I had noticed that she had always cast a glance over the grounds before getting into the car. I never asked her what she was thinking.

A Life

My mother's death certificate
was photocopied hanging
awkwardly on the machine.
The black ink of officialdom
took five of the eleven entries
encompassing her life statistically.
Female widow, 85 years,
'Retired' shop worker.
The starkness hurt.
Smiling I hear your
wry caustic comments.

7

FROM ANOTHER PLANET

Suddenly our encompassed little world was disturbed by a new and very strange phenomenon. Shortly before Christmas, former residents of the town who had emigrated to England began to reappear. Nothing unusual in that, but these were all dressed in a most peculiar fashion. There had been some vague talk about Teddy Boys and some of the British films featuring Tommy Steele and Lonnie Donegan gave a glimpse of this new breed, with rather strange forms of dress for young males. None of these fleeting film images or the vague talk of fashion had sunk into our consciousness.

Provincial Ireland was not ready for the arrival of the Irish version when the B & I boats disgorged a not inconsiderable number. It caused a major sensation. I can remember the first apparition that I saw on Mitchell Street: a thin, scrawny fellow who had passed our door every day on his way to the local factory before emigrating.

Here he was home, but like a character from another planet, dressed in an Edwardian type jacket with a velvet collar; a white pleated shirt and a black string tie; dark, very tight drainpipe trousers over bright pink socks and suede shoes with thick crepe souls: the real thing was so much better than the films. Hairstyles finished off the outrageous gear, usually a well-oiled mop tapering off into a 'DA'.

In spite of the gear I recognised Larry instantly. Although he was a few classes ahead of me and had left school at primary level, I knew him and we exchanged the usual strange country-type salute of 'Well', but I didn't know what to say when he came up the street. He kind of smirked, maybe unsure of himself also, but later I came to realise that anyone brave enough to tog himself out so outrageously would not be too bothered about acknowledging me. He probably was amused to see my unconcealed amazement. I just couldn't wait to share the news.

It was the big topic, particularly for those of us who were young but eager to engage with the real world. It wasn't quite an invasion on that Christmas in the 1950s, but as they were well spread out over the town one got the impression that they were all over the place. A few had acquired new accents that were indescribable and certainly incomprehensible, but these faded; maybe they just wised up. Somehow the flat Munster accents did not go with the gear.

All these guys had emigrated in dribs and drabs over the previous five or six years and were reasonably well established in Paddies Land; some had come home already on holidays.

They came into their own in the dance hall – most of them were expert 'jivers'. The local girls were a little hesitant to chance the fancy steps, but they got over their shyness pretty quickly. The stories were good from the crowded hops over Christmas, and the Teds, as they became known, almost re-created the local dancing scene. I remember being mesmerised by the parade into the local ballroom and feeling very deprived at being excluded on age grounds.

The weekend dances lasted from 9 p.m. to 3 a.m. in those days and there wasn't a hope in hell of admittance for any of us, even if we had the money. Life seemed very unfair then. Some people thought the Teds might have been refused admission, but that didn't happen. There was hardly any trouble apart from a few minor skirmishes with local guys who were jealous of the attention the Teds were getting from the local girls.

I was not surprised when in the middle of a class one of the Christian Brothers raised the 'visions on our streets'. He asked what we thought of them. It was all carefully orchestrated, just like everything he did. We were reticent enough, but he zoned in on a number and asked for our opinions. Most of these guys had left school at fourteen or fifteen or even earlier, and he emphasised the manner in which they were now the talk of the town because of the way they dressed. Most of us saw his point, but swapping places with them for a few weeks seemed a very attractive proposition. His closing comment was typical: 'Some of you scholars might make good candidates.'

Of course the phenomenon didn't last very long; it seemed to fizzle out after a year or so and it was a Christmas thing. Most of the lads, it was rumoured, were not too unhappy going back to Paddies Land. Stories emerged about their families being embarrassed by the spotlight, and this was understandable. Some middle-aged people had vague feelings of unease without being able to articulate them. Our next-door neighbour summed it up for many: 'Frankie, what's the world coming to, I ask you?'

I still retain a genuine feeling of warmth for the Teds. They were pioneers in their own way, and it did take a lot of courage to face the small town mentality dressed like fops, as they were described. Sociologists would later say these apparitions represented the first face of British youth culture, which grew out of post-war austerity. Fancy phrases never matched the fancy dress that appeared on the streets of our town in the mid-1950s.

8

THE LAST CREW

There was awareness from the start of 1956 that everything would be different once the Leaving Cert was finished. A certain vagueness existed about what exactly would transpire, but the expectation of freedom from studying, or the little of it that I was doing, added to the anticipated joy of liberation.

'Media' pressure was unknown; the points system for university entrance was as yet undiscovered. Only those who came from families that could afford it or the recipients of County Council scholarships went to university. Certainly I was not in the first category and had more or less ruled myself out of the latter by my indolence. Career guidance was almost non-existent, except that which may have been offered by individual teachers. I have no recollection of having received any particular advice. Was I seen as beyond it or was I just not listening?

This was an era before the introduction of Irish television, and Radio Éireann only broadcast at intervals for a few hours each day. Luckily there was Radio Luxembourg, which offered a continuous diet of pop music. This was a joyful, carefree period and surprisingly I felt something of that sense of privilege then.

I made one serious attempt to reach the great beckoning world beyond the Irish Sea, commonly called 'Blighty'.

The moment the bus pulled in to the station I knew this was my last chance. Seven were leaving, heading for London via the Rosslare to Fishguard route. One more body would not make a great difference. Several groups had left over the previous two years, almost denuding the locality. These were first timers with the exception of Freddie, who was a natural leader with a few years already served in England.

I had completed the Leaving Certificate and it seemed the perfect time to go and earn a few pounds during the holidays. After endless days of pleading with my parents, an immovable mountain of misunderstanding separated us. The answer was always the same.

'You have to sit the Civil Service and County Council exams and whatever else appears. How do you think you'll get a job?'

The author's parents, Peggy and Davey Marshall

It was almost impossible to get one, and I had no acceptable answer. It was hard as I watched all the preparation and listened to the chat. I went to Freddie and explained that I had the fare. He cut me short.

'No way Sunshine, your old lady would be dug out of me, anyway who would stake you until you got a job?'

I often wonder what would have happened if they had agreed. Would I have come back? It was pointless and I knew it, but I thought that I could pull it off on the night. Maybe if it had been planned a little better, but it was a huge disappointment. It was painful as I watched the lads boarding the bus, all apparently excited; no sign of regret about leaving.

It was always the same — everyone else could head off but I had all these bloody reasons that prevented me from heading. It was unfair, but there was nothing I could do.

There was a huge gang of well-wishers; only the parents were stony faced. Freddie reassured them all. He shook hands with each individual parent and told them they had nothing to worry about. It seemed a very thoughtful gesture.

There was no one to see him off. He didn't appear concerned.

In a flash they were gone. The old green CIE bus, covered in dirt, belched its way up the street and away down the Waterford Road. One more cargo of excited and expectant young men alive with the exaggerated yarns of the veterans; tales of Kilburn and Camden Town swallowed whole. One refrain lingers still, an utterance by one of the travellers: 'Are all the birds in Blighty blondes or what?'

It sounds daft, and clearly was then also, but it reveals a naiveté beyond belief.

9

PARTIAL FREEDOM

Having failed to escape with Freddie's gang heading for Paddies Land, I settled in to enjoying my good fortune as a junior member of the 'Island' (Clonmel Rowing Club). It was easy enough to get on with the life it offered. The club was at the top of the town, approached through a narrow laneway. Almost physically severed from the town, it seems that it was a place with which the ordinary folk did not concern themselves too much.

My Dad was enlightened enough to join the club in the early 1950s, and it was not exactly overrun by postmen. Bank clerks and local government officials made up the membership in the main, coupled with business people of course. A thriving junior section had blossomed from about 1953. The facilities included three tennis courts that we maintained ourselves, and table tennis in the pavilion for the wet days. We had swimming in the Suir with the luxury of dressing rooms. We had access to rowing boats, strangely called 'pleasure boats', to mess about on the river: a misnomer certainly.

Those delicious creatures of inexpressible beauty with long hair and skirts were an added attraction. Looking back without any tinted spectacles, they took up a huge part of our time. The amount of energy we expended in getting their attention never fails to puzzle me even now. A few of them were totally uninterested in our activities or pretended to be, and this was all part of the game. Naiveté is what most of the males displayed. It is easy to romanticise all this with hindsight, but it did exist. I am not sure if the rest of the junior members – about twenty – would look back with such longing. It was strange but delightful to hear Sr M. Anthony of the Poor Clare convent in Galway speaking on the Miriam O'Callaghan radio show in December 2012 of her special memories of that time in the Island.

Group pictured at the Tipperary Open Table Tennis Championships held in the Collins Hall in 1954 which was won by Kevin Pyke, Clonmel, who beat Tom Seacy, the former Irish international from Cork in the final. Included in the picture are Tom Seacy, Don Binchy, The Mayor Councillor Mick Kilkelly, Kevin Pyke, John Christie, Paddy Condon, Noel Reid, Billy Ryan, Tommy Leech, Jimmy Cummins, Jodie Collins, John Noonan, Dominic Kavanagh, Tom Stanley, Enda O'Riordan, Joe Burke, Jimmy Collins, Joe Pyke, Jim Strappe, Paddy Mullins, Mick Strappe and Frank Marshall.

Table tennis enthusiasts, 1954 (author is at back, on right)

The Island gang, 1955 (author at front centre)

What more could an eighteen-year-old expect from life? Spending a few hours there most days, it was astonishing that there was so much available, and we probably took it all for granted then. Years later in Dublin, talking about this period, there was an incredulous response as if Clonmel had been singularly blessed to have had this club. Of course there is the other relevant question – why did the club fade away as a social outlet? There was some activity in competitive rowing, but very little that involved others. A beautiful peaceful setting on a very gentle stretch of the river and overlooked by the Comeragh mountains. It was undoubtedly seen as somehow elitist by many of the ordinary townfolk.

It was all almost unsupervised except for a good-humoured caretaker, Bill, an Englishman who shared his fags with some of us at times. Most of us smoked incessantly when we could get the fags. There was no drinking: alcohol just didn't feature for juniors.

Smoking caused some problems when a few of us began rowing with serious intent. In the mid-1950s there was a resurgence of interest in rowing when a senior crew from the club scored a number of successes at regattas around the country. These senior oarsmen were emulated by a highly successful schoolboy crew. In 1956 the mantle passed to a new crew in a beautiful craft which had been recently acquired. We raced in Carlow and it was enjoyable but unremarkable. Amazingly I still have the 'Competitors' badge bearing the imprint of the club crest.

Serious training was undertaken under the eagle-eyed John Murphy, himself an accomplished oarsman. Lorcan Mullally was involved in the training also, as well as David Stapleton, Michael Moran, Michael Carey, Billy Dunphy, Eldon Morris (RIP), Gerry O'Donnell and myself. On a rain-lashed windy day with very choppy waters into which one of the race officials fell from a stake boat, we were less than distinguished, finishing a very poor last.

At an exhibition in 2007 to commemorate the Royal Showband, I came across the poster advertising that regatta on 26 July 1956. It stated that 'Visiting Crews will attend the Dance.' I have no recollection of attending the Olympic Ballroom on the night in question: maybe we were not considered a great attraction at the time. In the way of things, we seemed to just fade away as oarsmen, or some of us did. There was no official inquiry into our poor performance. It did provide a taste of the commitment needed to participate as serious competitors. Also, that senior crew provided great role models at the time and it was good to be exposed to them, but the addiction to the fags made it a very hard slog for a few of us.

One of the most memorable personal events was the day Tony 'Slim' O'Brien (RIP) and myself decided to dive from the Convent Bridge, which was quite a height over the Suir. We did it twice in quick succession, but I jumped and 'Slim' dived just like Tarzan. The Ma had been informed of my bravado while shopping long before I reached home. One other personal claim to fame, or possibly infamy, was my feat of cycling into the river fully clothed for the princely sum of ten shillings. A change of clothes was collected before the event. Nothing compares to the spectacular feats of Peter Dougan, who ran from the roof of the old clubhouse and dived into the river, accelerating and becoming airborne almost like Superman without the uniform. This was a rare if spectacular event, but he regularly performed on the diving boards just for the sheer hell of it.

The author cycling into the River Suir for a ten-shilling bet

The Leaving results did not emerge until early August, and it was easy to defer the day of Judgement. There was one break from the routine: a trip to Dublin courtesy of Córas Iompair Éireann, where seven of us from the Leaving class sat the entrance exam for clerkships in the company. I do not recall anything about the examination, but what has been an ineradicable memory over the years is that all seven of us trooped into the Carlton Cinema in O'Connell Street where the film *Rock around the Clock*, featuring Bill Haley and the Comets, was showing. Eamonn Lonergan, Ger and Joe Murphy, Jim Mara, Joe Hannon, John O'Keeffe and I made the big entrance.

One other trip was made to Dublin in July '56 and it lasted a few days. I was among the huge throng of 800 hopefuls spread around various locations – I was in Bolton Street Tech – sitting the competitive exam for the Clerical Officer jobs in the Civil Service. That turned out to be a rather significant event. It was a golden era, with or without the rose-coloured spectacles.

A poem of mine which was published in the Centenary Record of Clonmel High School (1998) was written and dedicated to Lieut.-General David Stapleton – a very prominent junior member in the Island – on the occasion of his appointment as Chief of Staff of the Defence Forces.

Leaving Cert class, 1956 (author second from left, front row)

Looking Back
(for Lieut.-General David Stapleton)

The Island in the barren fifties
a haven in a stagnant Clonmel
frenzied but harmless teenage activity
lean athletic leader, footballer supreme
idolized by all the females,
envied by some of the males.
Casual, confident but cagey at times
but always sound. No sign
of all that was to come.
What takes on to the pinnacle?
Ambition, ability, cunning, vision
Strength, weaknesses and even luck.
Is it the way things are destined?
Or are there hidden factors
mere mortals rarely see or feel?
Who knows apart from the one
and probably God.

10

THE AFTERMATH

It was very dark; the Pavilion seemed unreal in the half light from a single unshaded bulb. There was none of the usual activity. It was September and the rowing season was officially finished: the Annual Regatta the previous week had closed it in some style. Three of us sat quietly wondering why the rest of the gang had failed to surface on what was supposed to be the last fling. We didn't hang about: even the Suir was strangely silent as we made our way out across the metal bridge. This stark change was a little unnerving; maybe I was about to be left behind. One of my female companions was returning to UCD to complete an Arts degree and the other was starting in a teacher training college.

It was an uneasy realisation to discover that maybe I had missed the boat. An unimpressive Leaving Cert left me with few options; my parents were very disappointed. The comment of a former Principal of the school: 'We expected an awful lot more from your son – he was even a scholarship hope.' When that was repeated it came as a crushing indictment of my real lack of endeavour, and it did very little to improve the atmosphere in the house. However, the alternative of returning to repeat was not seriously considered.

It seemed inevitable that I would enrol in the local technical school. My first impression there was less than comforting. At almost eighteen I was two or three years older than most of the class. It was mixed in every sense of the word – most of the class were girls. It was back in senior infants that I had last shared a classroom with the opposite sex. An even bigger adjustment was the discovery that many of the teachers were females. It was a transformative experience, challenging but essentially enjoyable. I began to grow up after the relative isolation of the all-male arena in the secondary school.

Jeff was the Irish teacher. A very rugged appearance concealed an unexpected impish sense of humour. An inspirational teacher, his style was essentially interactive and the classes consisted of a series of dialogues and stories, all tempered with humour and sharp social comment. His energy, both mental and physical, was remarkable as he was not a young man. Some of the younger girls were very short on Irish vocabulary but he involved them with a bilingual approach. Most of them responded, and of course some charmed him. This was a real awakening for me.

Having secured the highest mark in Irish in the Leaving Cert class, I was relatively at ease in this class and the new experience nurtured a healthier attitude to the Irish language.

Shorthand and typing skills were taught by the captivating and commanding Miss Annie. It was a riveting experience to be confronted by this very attractive and extremely well dressed lady of indeterminate age, maybe somewhere in her forties. She stood there like an uncrowned queen, never in the same outfit on any two days. We were instructed conscientiously in the skills, but there was no choice – either it was her way or *slán abhaile*. Though not quite terrified I was overawed by her, but I had great respect for her skills and dedication.

She is remembered constantly; even as I type this piece I can hear her voice ringing out, boldly exhorting us: 'Stop looking at the keyboard; keep your eyes on the page!'

It was exclaimed as she pounded a wooden stick on the desk. Rhythmically.

Walter, a charismatic Cork man, taught art with great flair. It was enjoyable and a great change from the dour struggle in the High School, where the art teacher was never intended for the profession and alienated many students. These classes were therapeutic and relaxing, really good fun.

It is difficult to resolve the apparent differences now, but it is important to stress that there was no real corporal punishment and all of the teachers both lay and religious, with one notable exception, were hard working and conscientious.

It was a kind of separateness that I always felt in spite of the fact that my results were always in the top part of the class, with the one exception of the Leaving. Also I played on the school football team and was a member of the athletics team.

It is very easy to take a superficial view of the apparent differences between the two schools. The technical school was run entirely by lay teachers. I was encouraged and recognised as having ability. Also I felt I had an identity in the tech and was recognised as a member of a known family in the town. In the secondary school we were known nearly always by our surnames, and that separateness between pupil and teacher was a constant feature.

That is as I remember it. It is possible that if the secondary regime had some warmth and tolerance, many of us might have flourished.

A slightly different version of this piece was published in the *Clonmel Nationalist* newspaper in September 2008. It went largely unnoticed. The 'silent response' sums it up, more or less. The attitude of some contemporaries said it all. In the immortal words of Daniel Lanois, 'This is what is.'

11

INTO THE FORTRESS

My father would have recognised the envelope, and as a postman he would have guessed what it contained. He woke me and gave it to me. It told me *as Gaeilge* that I had been successful in the Civil Service examination, and it offered me the honourable position of Departmental Clerical Officer in the Office of the Revenue Commissioners. He was ecstatic. My heart sank.

Seven glorious months in the *Nationalist* newspaper office as a proofreader and subsequently doubling as a clerk was close to paradise, and I would have swept floors there, I was so content. Also I had fallen madly in love with Kitty, a redhead who was just gorgeous. I was more than fully occupied playing football and competitive table tennis. Dublin held no attraction.

My murmurings of discontent were ignored. I was taken to see the Editor of the newspaper. He had been suitably briefed.

'Look, Frank, when the next vacancy arises for a trainee reporter, and that may not occur for years, you will be considered only after the Directors' families. No one will be too impressed that you have reported on a few junior football matches and that you write the table tennis notes. You can't ignore this great chance in the Civil Service.'

That was it; my fate was sealed without any discussion. I felt I had been sentenced.

On 9 July 1957, having passed a medical examination and an Oral Irish interview, I walked into the Custom House in Dublin in search of Personnel Branch. Having signed a sheaf of forms including one on the Official Secrets Act, there was a brief introduction in a very large office to a sad-faced man who barely glanced in my direction. He set the official warm tone of welcome.

I was dispatched to the Foreign Parcel Post Depot at 100 Amiens Street, commonly called 'the FPP', just a stone's throw from Connolly Station – a two-storey red-brick building covered in grime in a less than salubrious area with a few small shops and some dingy and unremarkable pubs; a number of private dwellings carved into innumerable bedsits completed the dismal picture.

The Foreign Parcel Post Depot

'What am I going to do with him? Why do you always send the shaggin' rookies here?' This was the Staff Officer, a small, bearded Mayo man talking to a colleague in the Custom House. I remember thinking that a dog would get a warmer welcome. He ushered me into an enormous room almost the size of a football pitch, and my heart sank. I will never forget the moment.

'This is the main Customs floor and the Post Office authorities are responsible for producing all mail from abroad for Customs examination here. Duty is assessed as appropriate and the parcels are then delivered by the Post Office.' That was my official instruction, but I did not realise it. The place was littered with metal skiffs, all half-full of parcels. These were being shunted around by men in long yellowish dust coats. The sunlight beamed in through the glass roof, revealing the floating dust which permeated every inch of the room. Along the wall on both sides of the room sat many more men, all wearing suits, with heaps of documents in front of them. There was a conversational hum but it was overridden by the banging of skiffs and parcels. There was a kind of staleness about everything.

I don't know how I looked, but I felt awful. I knew I had made a dreadful mistake. Since the inception of the State I was probably the most disillusioned new entrant. Being inducted as the most junior Departmental Clerical Officer in the Customs and Excise, without too much ceremony or civility, was a huge shock. The reception in the 'FPP' was dreadful beyond words, and bewildering.

The Staff Officer took me to the end of this enormous room and introduced me to two men, one of whom just looked and continued writing without a word. The second man smiled and welcomed me.

'At last we have a young fellow in the Carding section.'

Dick turned out to be a Cork man – a small, cheerful man who was a temporary clerk; a fine decent soul, as emerged pretty soon. My work for the moment was explained in sixty seconds.

'All you have to do is copy the name and address on each parcel into that booklet: show the sender's name as well. It is a detention record and is done in triplicate. The tricky part is that you have to give a reason for detaining the parcel. Christy here will tell you all that if it's not written on it. Won't you, Christy?'

'I will in me arse – that's not my job. I work in the effin' Post Office not the bloody Customs.'

'It's all right, son, I'll put you right on all that; don't mind that latchico, he's only getting it up for you.'

Dick's intervention was necessary, as I was beginning to wonder what the hell was happening. It was all too much to absorb.

Christy was an elderly postman and his uniform had seen better days, as indeed he himself had. His breathing was a lot less than regular, and he had a cigarette butt cupped in his hand under the table. His next utterance contained a string of four-letter words bemoaning that he was now facing the struggle of lifting parcels for the rest of the day to keep me gainfully employed.

'Suppose you're another bloody culchie?'

My smiling assent produced a few more oaths.

'That's your official Post Office welcome, my boy.' Dick's tone of resignation conveyed his disapproval.

That was a moment which remained with me for a long time. Looking around that huge, noisy, dust-filled room surrounded by a throng of serious-faced strangers, I knew that I had made a monumental mistake in leaving the newspaper and all that Clonmel offered. It was a horrible sinking feeling.

It turned into a long, tedious day – the first of many – but eventually it came to an end. I had to walk up Talbot Street to O'Connell Street and queue for the no. 13 bus. The journey back to my cousin's house took almost an hour: a slow, grinding peak-time crawl during which I nodded off constantly with a sickening neck-jumping routine.

It was almost a fitting end to my first inglorious day in the Civil Service.

12

ADJUSTING

It was a lengthy queue outside the Savoy cinema, stretching way down O'Connell Street. All of us parked neatly on the edge of the wide footpath, enabling us to observe the pedestrians moving freely up and down the busiest street in the country. I didn't know a single soul. I was alone, surrounded by couples, many holding hands – some cheerful and talkative, others silent. It was a new experience to be on my own in a cinema queue, almost a painful recognition of the reality of city life.

A stark, disturbing reminder of Mickey the usher in the Ritz cinema in Clonmel: usually he had words of recognition for many in the queue, and inevitably much mockery and banter for others. His comments were priceless, and there was the occasional gem of cruel humour aimed at those who were singled out. That was almost an honour, and the mocking, derisive roars from the crowd could be heard way up the street. The recollection of those scenes was too much. Surprised by the offer of a single seat, I escaped into the anonymity of the cinema.

The morning routine was also a huge shock. It was a six mile slog on the bike – almost an hour in heavy traffic, pedalling furiously, often in lousy weather, to make it for 9 a.m. The ten minute stroll to the office at home often came back to haunt me as I waited impatiently at the Five Lamps traffic lights, wondering if I would make it on time. None of this was foreseen or even remotely imagined before I left home. Often I felt miserable during the first month or two. Opting out and going back home was not really the answer, as it would have been intolerable facing the questions. I would probably have finished up in Paddies Land. This was a momentous change in such a short few weeks.

Life drifted on. I was staying with my cousin, Meta, who was great fun and we got on well, but she was taken up with her two-year-old son. Her husband Johnnie was a quiet, thoughtful man and he plied me with fags, which were more than welcome. He took me to mass and Croke Park at weekends on a regular basis, on the back of his motor bike, a 500 cc Norton. It was wildly exciting when he got a chance to open it up. He was the first person to treat me as an adult.

After a few weeks I got to know some of the younger staff in the office. My cards were marked and I realised that it was not as bad as it seemed initially. Fergal played football for the Civil Service GAA club. He took me out to their club in Islandbridge. Significantly we had arranged to meet at the Gough Monument in the Phoenix Park. Most of it had disappeared when I arrived: the previous night the IRA had blown it into smithereens. Their campaign of the 1950s was swinging into gear.

My involvement with the Dublin Gaelic football scene was a short, inglorious one – a Junior match against the East Wall which was abandoned shortly after half time with three players already sent off. That was it. I had played Munster Colleges competitions and for Clonmel Commercials, winning a County Minor medal and a trial for the county team in 1956. There was no future in that savage cauldron, and the reassurances of the selectors sounded hollow.

Clonmel Commercials, Tipperary County Minor Champions 1955 (author is at back, third from right)

Listening to me moaning about this experience some time later in the office, 'Gero', a decent Dub from Ballyfermot and a fanatical supporter of Shamrock Rovers, invited me to play for Clover Rovers, a Junior soccer team he had brought together to play in the Leinster Leagues. Unable to use the 'Shamrock' name, he had settled in a most inventive manner for the next best description. I played in the inaugural game at centre forward and had the honour of being the first man to kick a ball for this team, which featured every week for over thirty years in the Leinster Leagues.

However, my soccer career was an equally undistinguished one. I had no experience of playing soccer apart from messing about on the streets at home, and the pivotal position of centre forward was way beyond my capacity. Also, playing in the wilds of the Phoenix Park in the middle of winter was less than pleasurable. Gero was unhappy but let me go reluctantly. Some months later one of the lads in the office congratulated me on my new-found fame: 'I see you're a regular scorer for Clover, with a hat trick last week.'

Someone was playing under my name – a common enough practice. Gero said it was a clerical error and smiled innocently. I bought the *Evening Press* on Tuesdays for a few weeks, but it seemed my career had petered out.

It was pretty clear even then that I had been spoilt with the conditions we had in Clonmel in the Island club. On another level it was hard to take on this regular commitment while unsettled in Dublin.

The most immediate problem was that on a weekly wage of six pounds net (there was a ten shilling deduction of income tax), I was chronically short of cash from about Wednesday. There was no problem in borrowing a pound or two, but I found it personally very difficult, almost degrading. The alternative was eating on the 'slate' in the canteen, but this left one in the egg and chips brigade. Settling the bill on the Friday, one was still short going into the next week.

I began to cop on that it was a question of adapting and making the best of things. Happily I was invited to join Charleville tennis club by Leslie Warren, where I played league table tennis and tennis. It was like reaching the 'Promised Land'. I played on the first team and we were successful in Division 3. I was selected to play for the Leinster League Team against a Munster selection on the basis of my results in the leagues.

Everything changed from then. I was enjoying myself, actively involved in the two racquet games, and I settled in the 'Big Smoke'. It was pretty clear that I was fortunate to have been based in the FPP, as I might not otherwise have got the invitations to become involved in sport. The experience and expertise picked up in the Island and the boys' clubs in the sports at home made an immeasurable difference.

Going home at Christmas was a huge joy, not having visited for four months – no five-day weeks then – and I enjoyed myself in spite of the fact that the 'love of my life', Kitty, had transferred her affections elsewhere. My cultured and verbally burning love letters were clearly ineffectual. It was a delightful break, and I appreciated my family more than ever, having missed them so much in the initial separation. However, I was also happy to return to what had become a very different but enjoyable existence.

13

SURVIVING IN THE FORTRESS

The phone rings in the Customs correspondence section of the FPP. Eddie Mac – an amiable but often disgruntled official in his fifties – answers, and shouts at the top of his voice: 'P.S. Ó Marascail!' (my official name in Irish), repeated twice, maybe twice again. I get up and walk the full length of the room to cheers and sometimes hand clapping, accompanied by derisory roars: 'Pay the woman or get out of the bed!'

This was not uncommon, but was often heard more on Thursdays or Fridays – pay days. The call could be official or personal and this racket would easily be picked up by the caller. I was not the only one singled out for this pantomime.

Imagine four men around two tables: two in long yellow work coats are postal sorters who open the parcels and present the contents to the Customs officer, who assesses the duty if applicable, and the contents are repacked and sorted. The charges are given to the Post Office clerk, who completes the operation with a docket affixed to each parcel. Two separate charge records are kept by Customs and Post Office. Slow, methodical and extremly tedious.

A particular group is recalled, one of whom appears just a little isolated at one side of the tables. Tommy doesn't wash, and the unimaginable pungent odour is pervasive. He talks incessantly in a rapid high-pitched Dublin accent. Extremely intelligent, he has opinions on everything under the sun. When the papal enclave had chosen John XXIII, I recall Tommy reenacting his version of a dithering candidate being urged by a forceful angel: 'Will you take the effin' job, John!' It was a lot more graphic, but in its own way harmless. The PO management had tried delicately to deal with the problem but failed.

Approached by the senior official – 'Tommy, the staff are talking about you' – the reply was curt: 'You should hear what they are saying about you.'

The problem only arose in one week out of four because of the rotation of duties in the PO. One affectionate memory of Tommy occurred on the rear steps of the Custom House, which open out on to a view of the Liffey, about 7.15 p.m. when a few of us were leaving after overtime. Tommy, on his way to a late duty and carrying his bundle of papers in a raincoat, stopped suddenly and exclaimed: 'Marshall, do you ever go home? I wouldn't mind but you'd never spend a tosser.'

The high-pitched laugh was the last sound I heard. One of the women in the group looked puzzled. 'Frank, how do you know him?' Her tone said it all ...

Approximately 70 officials were engaged in various forms of the above procedures, others interacting on the telephone and some attending to callers to the public office. The noise and the dust were impossible to ignore, but one got used to the implacable din over a period. It was a very lively and unusual scene, and in spite of the opening examples most people just got on with their work in a normal, competent manner. I learned to live with it.

Some of the officials in both departments were the brightest and most learned men that I had encountered. Once engaged on a good day, discussions on literature and politics were stimulating. I learned about the Spanish Civil War and the pogroms against the Jewish people in Limerick and Cork. Our own Civil War was also a topic, if often *sotto voce*, as some of the staff had actually participated. Sport of all descriptions was always a reliable topic, leading to many a heated debate. This was in the course of assessing duty on anything up to a hundred or more parcels.

A small number of the Customs staff had transferred from the British service at the time of Independence in 1922, having worked in Excise distilleries and spirit warehouses in the UK. It was difficult for some of them to adapt to their diminished status in the FPP.

The absence of women was striking, yet not unsurprisingly they were discussed more frequently than almost any other topic. There was always a sexual braggart around, relentlessly pursuing an audience. The official view on the absence of women, rarely expressed, was that it would be too costly to provide separate toilet facilities for females, so they were spared the experience of serving in this weird and challenging place.

Some of the staff from both departments had arrived in the FPP on disciplinary transfers due to chronic sick leave records and incessant late attendances. The place was often referred to as 'The Sanatorium', and of course these difficulties were not miraculously cured on arrival in Amiens Street. It was seen in some official circles as a refuge for people with alcohol problems. This applied to a small number, but it was obvious at times that some were inebriated quite early in the day. The 'early opening houses' were located quite near Amiens Street. Also some managed to negotiate credit facilities in the local pubs, but these arrangements never lasted too long.

One part of my work for quite a while was dealing with personnel matters – staff leave applications and sick leave returns – on behalf of the Senior Staff Officer. It led to constant interaction with all grades, even to handing out salary cheques when they arrived. It happened twice that they failed to appear, which resulted in consternation. Special arrangements had to be made to have cash facilities available in the Custom House. The missing cheques never surfaced, nor was it satisfactorily explained how they disappeared between Pearse Street Sorting Office and Amiens Street. A very senior PO official told me much later that it was almost certain that a disgruntled postman had simply thrown them in the Liffey because he had been insulted by 'a drunken Customs officer'.

It sounds daft, but at the time I accepted it as a possibility. It was not all sweetness and light between the multiplicity of grades in the two departments, which led to some petty official snobbery. It was grim, but it was confined to a small number of malcontents. With the provocation that I witnessed occasionally, I could see an injured soul suddenly deciding to fling a bag into the Liffey as the sight of the grey, monstrous Customs House loomed up on Butt Bridge.

Many of the officials were based in the FPP by choice, as they lived on the north side of the city and it was pure convenience.

'I wouldn't hang around this kip for very long, young fellow; there is a stigma attached to it, if you know what I mean?' It was true of course, but there were few choices open at that time.

It seemed that the Custom House was the place to be noticed. Both sexes were represented, and it operated on a different plane. People dressed differently, and many spoke a strangely refined dialect. It was pointed out to me that slouching in official chairs was not recommended. My response to the female Staff Officer was that I had not been instructed in the art of sitting in a public office and was not aware of where the relevant instructions were contained.

Her shocked expression told me it was a pointless and rather stupid remark, even if provoked by her own haughty tone. I found myself dispatched back to Amiens again. At nineteen I was less than concerned, but it was evident that I had a lot of learning to do. My colleague Dick smiled as he forecast: 'You're not destined for the top in this job, Frankie Boy.'

The contrasts between the two locations were easily seen even then, but the regime in the Custom House was not unlike any normal Civil Service office; it had its routine and a veneer that was distinctly absent in the wilderness of the FPP.

Over a number of years I volunteered for relief work in the provincial offices and escaped temporarily, but always ended back in the prison of the FPP until finally freed on promotion in 1967.

14

SUIT FOR THE MUNSTER FINAL

'What are you going on about? Didn't I tell you that all Tipp men are exempt from mass on the day of the Munster Final?'

It was my friend Mac, also from Tipperary. He said it with an air of infallibility as if it were a decree from the Vatican. It was 1958, right in the middle of the era of religious obligations.

On Sunday morning I cycled to what was then called Kingsbridge Station in my clerical grey suit. Most of the qualms of conscience had been dispelled …

It was almost an all-male crowd on the train to Thurles, all wearing suits – casual gear as such was almost unknown. Very few women travelled to matches then. The game was the main topic. Television had not arrived officially here, so the newspapers were devoured, but coverage was limited to one or two articles. Every possible eventuality was played out in the small eight-seater compartments.

I met with my father and his friend Mikey Brett in Liberty Square. They had travelled over on the train from Clonmel. My father was genuinely glad to see me.

'You're looking very well.'

He launched into a series of questions about 'the Job'. My position as a Departmental Clerical Officer in the civil service was one from which he derived immense pride and about which he had an insatiable curiosity. He was unaware that I was less than impressed with my position. My father saw Clerical Officers on a par with the Post Office Inspectors.

It was just over a year since I'd left home to join these dizzy heights, as he viewed them, and I was aware of his keen eye of appraisal. Mikey was more direct: 'God yer all decked out in the new suit, the Big Smoke must be agreeing with ya.'

Smiling, I left them to get a large bottle of lemonade. They were both well armed with sandwiches and flasks of tea. As I rejoined them I overheard Mikey's strong south Tipperary accent: 'God, Davey didn't he get on fierce well in Dublin, sure that suit must have cost a fortune.'

They wouldn't have noticed my blushes as we moved off as part of the huge throng slowly edging its way towards the hurling ground.

My father was a quiet man. It was only when I left home that it began to dawn on me just how much he had been affected by the loss of his two brothers, Frankie and Christy, in a drowning accident in 1951 in Clonea, Co. Waterford. He himself was fortunate to survive on that day. He carried the effects of the trauma quite stoically, and it was not easy to see the real effects of the tragedy.

The subject of hurling was the exception that allowed him to be re-energised. It was strange to see him gripped with such fervour. The words just poured out of him. This was the man who in the early 1930s borrowed his brother Paddy's new bike and cycled to Ballybrophy – over fifty miles – to connect with the Cork train *en route* to Croke Park, where Kilkenny were in action. Returning on the train the same day, he faced the cycle from Ballybrophy back home to Clonmel. Paddy remembers him putting a large bottle of lemonade on his head and draining it almost in one swallow. His normal twenty-six-mile cycle as a country postman the following day was apparently no more trouble than usual.

The author's father (right) and Uncle Paddy

Paddy Marshall at the Ollie Walsh memorial statue, Thomastown, Co. Kilkenny

No matter in what tone this story is narrated, it suggests a passion that was very rare. That same unswerving devotion to Kilkenny hurling cost him a dearly in the 1950s and '60s with the dominance of Tipperary. My father's colleagues in the Post Office mocked him mercilessly if good-humouredly, but his far too serious attitude was a heavy burden to carry even in that not too turbulent cauldron. All the fascination with Kilkenny was far from my mind that day as I recalled the saga of the 'new suit'.

Six pounds a week as a Clerical Officer didn't leave much scope for suit buying. I discovered that most of my colleagues used the hire purchase system, or 'the never never', as it was known. This was an era long before credit cards were known in Ireland. Amazingly, these cards later disposed of the social stigma attached to buying on credit. I was dispatched to a well-known store that operated the system. After a ten-day wait, my application was refused in three terse lines.

No reason was given, and my appeal was not even considered. I was certain that the woman with whom I dealt just didn't like the look of me, and I was foolish enough to say as much in the office. The development of the story by one of the funny men left nothing to the imagination. I found a smaller shop which approved my application, but not before one of my colleagues had forged my father's signature as guarantor.

There was one small snag. The approval meant that a letter had been issued to my father requesting written confirmation of his willingness to act as guarantor. This was totally unexpected. My father complied, and the store went ahead with the deal. I was worried about the forged signature. All my fretting was unnecessary: no one in the shop said a word, and my father never mentioned it. Hurling was his primary concern that day.

Every week I trotted in to pay my instalment of five shillings (thirty-two cents in current coinage). It took ages to pay off the debt.

Mikey would be amazed now that suits are very often acquired on the 'never never' with a credit card but are normally worn only in the VIP section, and that a ticket would now devour about two months of his pay then.

Thousands of women supporters among the faithful would be the biggest shock of all. His comments would be worth recording.

Hurling was not my father's only passion, and a poem I wrote that was published in *Reality* magazine, in the opinion of a few people, caught the essential nature of the man. Subsequently while studying for a diploma in theology in the Milltown Institute, I used the poem as basis for exploring the nature of 'Faith'.

Faith Journeys

Your smiling gentle face in 1969 photographed on Tramore beach.
A tentative restraining hand touches your eldest grandson
as he glares at his younger brother, cradled by you,
protecting this errant two-year-old sand thrower.
My lasting impression of you, reconciling, enjoying your role.
A serious but fair and generous man, like the God
you worshipped with unfailing regularity and commitment.
Daily mass at seven before your grinding twenty-six-mile cycle
delivering mail to an eager, welcoming people.
You shepherded annually to Knock Shrine in a
Legion of Mary Pilgrimage train, reciting rosaries
in packed carriages. It seemed your lips never ceased
beseeching Jesus and Mary for endless favours
for others and so much else that I knew
nothing of nor cared about then.

Peacemaker: the author's father and two sons, Kevin and David, on Tramore beach

15

REQUIEM FOR A MONK

It was February 1962 and I was staying in the Cistercian Monastery of Mount Melleray in the middle of the Knockmealdown Mountains in County Waterford. In January I had been relieved of my right kidney in the Mater Hospital in Dublin after a succession of wearying tests and exploratory operations. The tedium of an enforced recovery period at home drew me to the monastery.

There was only one other guest present: a mildly eccentric Englishman who was a skilled organist, a talent he demonstrated in the church during the week. One of the elderly monks died suddenly and we were both invited to attend the obsequies. The requiem mass was celebrated by the Abbot. The solemn chanting created an eerie atmosphere, heightened by the presence of the deceased monk on a catafalque flanked by four very large candles in the centre aisle.

At the end of mass the Abbot, preceded by the cross bearer and two servers, approached the remains of the monk and began to chant the prayers for the departed. The firm, resonant voice, betraying no emotion, penetrated every inch of the church. The slow inevitable journey to the graveside began. The Abbot was followed by the community chanting the Canticle of Zachary; the sound of 'Benedictus Dominus Deus Israel …' reverberated beautifully as they moved gently through the dimly lit cloisters, followed by the four pall bearers carrying the body of the deceased monk on his last journey.

As I followed this impressively dignified group, my mind was awash with a mass of unprocessed thoughts about the dedicated life of the deceased, which was confined within these narrow passages for over sixty years. Leave to return home for the funeral of a close family member was not allowed. Total silence dominated the Rule of St Benedict and sign language was the norm within a day that commenced at 2 a.m. It was divided between prayer and work and featured a very restricted diet.

As we entered the cemetery, the cold biting wind off the mountain slopes helped to focus my thoughts. The open grave was blessed and sprinkled with holy water by the Abbot. He then incensed the remains which lay on the catafalque. Only at that moment did it really strike me.

There was no coffin. The Abbot's slow, mournful chant as he intoned the Antiphon rang out; the choir's response was caught in the wind and the sound seemed to taper off.

An awkward silence hung in the air; most eyes were downcast. The feeling of expectancy was palpable. A small monk threw back his cowl and stepped forward to the graveside. The silence continued as I saw one monk beckon to a colleague, who responded with a slight but definite shake of his head. Suddenly four monks were standing at the graveside; two climbed down into the grave and then the body of the deceased was lifted and cautiously handed down to the others. Clad in his habit and boots, he was laid in the grave. Some straw was passed down to cover the remains.

After a short pause a shovel was handed to the Abbot, who placed two shovelfuls of clay in the grave. The usual familiar thud of clay on a coffin was not heard. The grave was filled in almost immediately, and the cortege returned in silence. There were no apparent signs of grief.

My own reaction was so mixed and confused that it took some time to absorb it all, but at lunch the other guest told me that he had got permission to play a tribute on the organ in the community chapel. Dutifully I sat as he thundered what sounded appropriate. Two monks looked in, smiled and left. Elgar's 'Dream of Gerontius', based on a poem by Cardinal Newman, was more than a little unfamiliar. Later I was to learn that it deals with the journey of a soul to Judgement.

I left the monastery two days later. The burial service, particularly the absence of a coffin, still bothered me. A friend arrived home from Dublin that weekend driving a borrowed Triumph Herald. His plans were on a slightly different plane. My concerns did not get much of an airing. So-called ordinary life does go on.

The practice of burial without a coffin was discontinued after Vatican 2, when it was decided that services should conform to those obtaining in the local communities.

16

TRYING TO ESCAPE

'Are you gone mad or what? That's crazy stuff, have you actually put it in?'

Reaching for his beloved pipe, Dick seemed genuinely bothered.

'Look, you need to be very sure of what you are at here. Is it a formal resignation, and where is it now?'

'It's on the Surveyor's desk, but he's not in yet.'

'Ah look, come on Frankie, any shagger can look at it there and it will be all over the office in a flash, and what will he say when he hears it from some cute hoor?'

I hadn't thought about that, but if I was resigning, well, what did it matter one way or the other? Now I was getting confused, having spent ages thinking about it. All Dick was doing was unsettling me, even though he meant well.

'Are you in some kind of bother, or is it those quare wans you met in London?'

Dick was in his sixties; his response was predictable. All his working life he had spent chasing the dream of permanency from the unreachable depths of a temporary clerkship ... For some reason he was never offered it, and he was not able to manage the Irish in the exams he sat. He believed passionately that his national service record during the War of Independence should have been enough, and this was a deeply troubling scourge, especially when he considered the elevation of some of his contemporaries in other areas. I knew it was a mistake to tell him: all I wanted to hear was 'Wise man – about time you got out of this kip!'

The pipe was going full belt at this stage; the first deep inhalations sent the smoke all the way to the immeasurable depths somewhere near his big toes.

Smoke never seemed to reappear from there unless he got lost in a bout of coughing.

'Do you want a fill?'

Smiling, I shook my head; he had introduced me to the pleasures of pipe smoking but I rarely bothered in the office. The interrogation began in earnest: what would my parents say? Where would I get a job? All predictable stuff.

Why the shagging hell did I tell him? Was I looking for this kind of response? It was driving me crazy.

'Look, Dick, I have to go: I'll see you later,

It was the first thing that entered my head, but it got me out of there.

As I walked up the main examination floor there was a strange unreality about the moment. The ubiquitous clouds of dust rising from all the mangy parcels that had survived the Atlantic crossing or the smaller Pond could be seen glistening in the streaming sunshine from the glass roof. There was a strange soundless quality: everyone was spouting away but I couldn't hear them. Just inside the door sat four of the most senior Custom officers, survivors of the British regime, all in their sixties, pontificating as always on matters as diverse as the Dead Sea Scrolls and the odds-on the favourite in the next race. All of it was being studiously ignored by their Post Office colleagues. If you sat in front of these elderly men day in, day out, they tended to repeat the same old stuff. Hence the expressionless, lifeless scene.

It was unreal and rather eerie, but the door banged in my face and it all reverted to some form of reality.

I knew I would have to get out of this maelstrom or end up like the four Horsemen of the Apocalypse, inside the door. Incessant, inconsequential chattering that was disregarded by everyone. Well, that was it. No one took any notice of anyone else unless there was some drama or scandal.

The darkened space between the public office and the main floor focused my attention and the voice of the Great White Chief, as he was called, boomed my name in Irish: 'Mr Ó Marascail an fear atá uaim.'

As always he wanted me for something or other, but he wasn't always in such good humour. A most unpredictable man, he detested his posting in the FPP as it didn't augur well for his future career. These near-lunchtime arrivals were interpreted by the cynics as 'late morning matinées with the wife' – an original phrase for his marital adventures in official time. As I followed him into his office I froze, as the single sheet bearing my resignation stood out in terrible isolation on his desk. As he picked it up I launched into Irish, telling him that I had changed my mind about applying for the Irish scholarship, and he was diverted in the act of concentrating on my comments.

As he began to focus I kept up the flow of Irish and I leaned over and gently took the sheet out of his outstretched hand. This was crazy stuff, but he just smiled and nodded: he was not concentrating. It was too close for comfort.

In a flash he told me what he wanted done, and I was gone. Sweating, I closed the door behind me. It was too close a call, but it was instinctive stuff. I knew it was not alone out of character for me, but also just what seemed right at that moment.

Later at lunchtime I headed on my bike for Dollymount: the stifling milieu of the GPO canteen would have been insufferable, but the loneliness of the open spaces surrounding the Bull Wall was not ideal either. A few old guys walking dogs. What was it about the old guys today? I couldn't avoid them. Gazing out on the calm, almost still water of Dublin Bay provided no inspiration of any kind. I had made a decision, and the first person to challenge it had unsettled me completely. My certainty was disappearing into the water ahead of me. All the questions raised by Dick were chasing each other around my skull. It was ridiculous to be confronted by all of this again after my decisive production of the single sheet of resignation.

'What will you do? Where will you stay?'

This was at the core of it. What did anyone do, that ever left this God-forsaken place? I knew that it boiled down to whether I would be better off in London. There was no easy answer, but at least there would be more opportunities, and anything would be better than remaining a Clerical Officer with no prospects. Of course the really unsettling thought was that I had missed the boat. Only two years previously Michael Moran, a friend from the Island days, had resigned his bank job and worked on a building site to earn his university fees. I was languishing in the Mater Hospital then. At this stage he was studying in Trinity. (His example was followed by Michael Ahearne and Anthony Meany from Clonmel. All three slaved on the building sites of London and earned their just rewards by graduating and going on to distinguished careers.)

I knew that it was not for me, but this nagging feeling remained. It led to many other questions, none of which were easily answered. Bollocks. Did it really have to be so tortuous – unendingly so?

The answer was not apparent sitting on the Bull Wall gazing into the water.

It was a slow, rather melancholy trip back in along the Clontarf road. The sight of the Fortress beyond the Five Lamps didn't raise my hopes one shagging bit.

17

LIFE IN DUBLIN 6

We were part of a rowdy crowd, mainly students. It was the Veterinary Students' Dress Dance in the Metropole Ballroom. Frank was about ten years older than me. We had been members of the Island Rowing Club, but he was an active oarsman. He left school without completing the normal span in secondary school. Qualified as an electrician, he worked in his uncle's electrical business.

'I know more than the whole gang of them about electrical engineering: seven years at it. I took two years on each year, and I'll have my degree this year; then we'll see who is a failure.' This is a much abbreviated version of his oration, which was colourfully embroidered. While well fortified with liquid nourishment, he was very focused. I can recall his conviction and passion. His determination was palpable that night, and I was very conscious of the general feeling among his contemporaries that he just wasn't bright enough. Before he left me he said he intended to study in the USA when he graduated. I didn't really believe him on the night.

In due course Frank got his degree and went and studied at Harvard Business School, where he got a Master's in Business Studies. He returned to Clonmel, and from his base in the old family electrical firm he broadened it into one of the biggest electrical contracting conglomerates operating across the world.

Years later I reminded him of our encounter in the Metropolis and he just smiled. He was a very generous benefactor of the Island Rowing Club over the years, and gave many hours coaching the rowing crews.

Dressing up for these shebangs was supposed to make the difference. A hired dress suit cost fifteen shillings. It always seemed a bit silly to me, but most of the dances were enjoyable: all one needed was the right attitude and of course the right partner; sometimes a few pints of beer made it all a bit more tolerable. It also gave the ladies the freedom to invite a partner to accompany them. The occasional invitation was magnificent and great for the auld ego.

I had moved from digs in Glasnevin, unceremoniously pushed by my landlady, who had seemingly tired of my presence and invented the unusual story that I was 'peeing' on the toilet floor. This was a source of much amusement to my fellow lodgers. Five men and I were blessed with the doubtful honour. I moved on. I made the big shift across the Liffey, never having lived on the South side, and ended up in a flat in Harold's Cross. Roger and Fintan – two decent Limerick men, sound technicians in RTE – were my flatmates. It turned out to be a spectacularly good move for me. The boys had a rare zest for life. No mere weekend socialising for them; it was like a merry-go-round all week. Limited funds restricted my movements.

Weekends were sometimes hectic. Regular visits of the gang to the Saturday night dance in Ashbrook Tennis Club were memorable; situations developed almost spontaneously and nearly everyone in sight ended up in our flat. Often I would be called into service to make up the numbers. The boys would return with a group of friends, including a few ladies. My regular Sunday pork chops would be cooked and devoured by some of the guests. One needed a sense of humour: once I discovered a couple rather neatly ensconced in my single bed when I came home. This was just too far down the road to freedom. I survived, but the deliciously perfumed odour on my pillow required an earlier than usual change of bed linen.

A more auspicious visitor was the British Labour MP Ian Mikardo. A friend of one of the lads was entertaining him as a business acquaintance. Sometimes a number of RTE people came back to the flat with the lads when they were working together on the late shifts. These visits were all very civilised compared to the weekend ones. We had a TV – rare in those days – a tape recorder, and unlimited records, mostly classical. Invitations to various functions and parties were common. Pitch and toss schools did not feature.

The big event, scheduled well in advance, was the RTE Dress Dance in 1962 in the Shelbourne Hotel. It was the first one, as the station had begun transmitting the previous year. I was promised two tickets. I invited my girlfriend, but the tickets were not produced until the day of the dance when it was impossible to contact her, she being a full-time student.

Urgent phone calls resulted in a different partner accompanying me. While I was in the balcony of the ballroom, Roger came up the stairs grinning: 'Do you know who is downstairs?'

He couldn't wait to tell me that my girlfriend was dancing around the floor with 'a bloody engineer' (most technicians were not in love with graduate engineers). I was dumbfounded, but of course it was true. I felt pretty miserable, maybe a bit ashamed of my own stupidity. All the gang thought it was hilarious. She had accepted the second invitation, and that was it. There were no awkward scenes but the relationship petered out soon after.

I lived in Harold's Cross for about three years; it was a carefree and uncomplicated period.

18

NEW FRONTIERS

There was much talk about interviews and promotion. Really too much for my liking. I wasn't eligible to compete, so it was irrelevant. This competition was to fill one vacancy as Staff Officer, so the majority were going to be disappointed. One candidate was fancied, and it seemed he was also universally unpopular. My work was mainly assisting him and he did a lot of the Staff Officers' work.

The prophets were right: he got the job, and was gone to Cork almost before half the staff knew. The subsequent anger was palpable, and all the frustration emerged over the next few weeks. There was much talk about the influence of the Knights of Columbanus; this was relevant but impossible to verify.

Out of the blue I was offered a great opportunity to escape. The wife of one of the staff suffered a crippling stroke, and her husband was allowed to return to Dublin on compassionate grounds. There was no queue of applicants in the week before Christmas. Subsistence and travel allowances were normally attractive. When the position was offered I jumped at the chance, and was on the train to Lifford within forty-eight hours.

'You are either running from a woman or a bookmaker; Donegal in December, come on, Tipp men don't usually make such crazy decisions.'

'Don't forget to subscribe to my send-off, Benny.'

His response was predictable and unprintable.

I got a fistful of money – just couldn't believe it. 'An Advance for Travelling Purposes', it was called. Thirty days at two pound a night and this was just to cover one month. It was more than six weeks' wages, and tax free as an allowance. I was in clover. The North West in December was a little less warm than the French Riviera, but I was out of Amiens Street. Freedom.

Accommodation had been arranged by one of the local staff. It was in Strabane, which meant that I was residing officially in Northern Ireland. One had to walk across the frontier from Lifford. Literally the bridge straddled the Border, which was mysteriously somewhere in the middle of the river. The cold was vicious and unsettling. I was tired, hungry and wondering what lay ahead, with no room for fanciful thoughts about Republican refugees swimming to safety in the swirling waters of the Foyle. A complete stranger accosted me as I set off to walk to my 'digs'.

In a very sharp, high-pitched Northern accent he asked if I knew where I was staying. Then he said: 'Are you a Customs man then?'

Eventually I relented and was told politely that the address to which I was going was not one that the Southern staff frequented.

He worked in the railway station as a porter. I was not prepared for any of this stuff. I almost yelled at him, but this was a strange client. He hung in with me all the way into Strabane.

'Thems are black Protestants so they are: I'll get you a house much cheaper and safer.'

I couldn't believe my ears. He stayed at my side until the good lady of the house opened the door. I was warmly greeted and the porter melted into the darkness.

It was the 'Black North', but the political scene had been relatively quiet since the ending of the IRA active campaign of the 1950s. I had no idea that this kind of naked sectarianism would appear in these circumstances. The centuries-old enmity was lurking just under the surface.

I was based in the railway station in Lifford: there was a fair amount of commercial traffic crossing the border. My job was processing the import documents. A good working knowledge of the regulations was necessary, but it was fairly regular traffic. Simple enough once the cash was in order. One could handle several thousand pounds in a day, but often it would be much more modest. My boss was tentative initially, but realised I was not exactly a neophyte.

'I'd say you know what you're about, but one word of advice – watch the cash; there are all sort of latchicoes coming and going here. Send it off every day, never hold it overnight. Keep the safe locked always.'

That was it – we got on fine, and argued long and hard about Edna O'Brien and other writers. I couldn't convince him that her books had any merit. He disliked Clare people. He was a grand man, and we never had a cross word. The really good news was that all the preventive uniformed staff – mostly young guys like myself – had cars and were happy to take me to the weekend dances: except one guy, and the word was that it would be better if I were not seen with him. He had a reputation. God, it was funny. I was enjoying myself, there was no pressure of any sort, it was a glorious unexpected change, and the women in Donegal were delightful.

'They will ate you up, Tipperary man, you'll never escape – either nurses from Altnagelvin or shagging teachers and county council clerks. All Fenians with a sprinkling of Prods; God I would love to swap with you.'

The boss's deep-seated laughter said it all. He really did envy me.

And so it went, but they didn't ate me up – well, not all of them. Six glorious months. It was a huge change from the relentless boredom of Amiens Street, dominated by interdepartmental rivalry and the corrosive cynicism and depressive attitudes of the wounded inmates. It was hard and bitterly cold weather, but I was amazed at how uncomplicated life had become. The work was hardly the most fulfilling, but the pleasant atmosphere made the difference.

It was strange to pass the same people every morning, and it was clear that they all knew who I was, what I did, and, as it turned out, my precise grade. Because of the large number of Customs guys who were married to locals they would be as familiar as I was with the grades and salary scales. It made no difference to me. Life was to be lived and enjoyed: this was the big discovery.

The weekends were full of fun; a few jars, a dance, many women. 'Borderland' held an enormous number of dancers. These chaps thought nothing of driving miles to other venues. Usually it all ended the same way: standing in doorways looking for small sexual favours. All denied, so the forecasts of my boss were overrated. He thought it all hilarious as I related my frustration, though it was often interspersed with some invented stuff.

'What about Edna O'Brien now?' he laughed.

Derry city on Saturday afternoons ... I even had a free pass on the train from Strabane. The book shops were the main attraction, and there was no end to my money with all the extra subsistence expenses. God but I was content. It didn't last. Greed shifted me in the end. I was filling a higher grade post, so I got the dreaded note.

Mr Ó Marascail, Please report to the Collector Dublin.

The good times were over. I look back with great affection on that short period: no hangovers of any kind, no regrets. It restored my belief in the auld job, and I think I was just a little wiser. Possibly.

19

CROSSWORDS

There was something not quite right about him. Maybe it was the absence of his glasses, and of course he was wearing a suit. Jim never wore a suit – at least not in the office. Always in that dirty brown leather jacket and the brown cavalry twill slacks that had seen better days. An open-neck shirt, which looked as if it was always the same one. It was mandatory to wear a tie in the office then, but it was only one of the many small things he ignored. He was past all that now. It was somehow deliciously ironic that for almost the first time in years he was well togged out, but his big old fat body was well framed in a dark brown coffin.

Two women stood on the other side of the coffin. Both were middle aged, well dressed; neither was in black. I was trying to figure out where they fitted in, and then a soft, questioning voice: 'Do you forgive him now, Mary?'

There was no immediate reply, but I heard a deep sigh and then a clear, steady response: 'No.'

'Are you sure, love?'

I was transfixed, and couldn't stop staring across the coffin: not quite sure, I guessed that one was probably Jim's former wife.

'He never thought he did anything wrong, so forgiveness makes no sense now; anyway it's all too long ago. I'm sorry I came: I knew all this stuff would be dragged up. O Good Jesus I have to get out of here.'

She turned and walked straight out. I wasn't sure how much of this was really apparent to the rest of the groups scattered around the morgue. It seemed appropriate, somehow, even in death that there was some unevenness. I could imagine how he might have responded. He had a way of sounding outraged. Then he would shift the glasses up off the bridge of his nose and give the usual derisive snort. Where were his glasses? So much had changed in a few hours.

Jim's marriage difficulties were well known in the office and there had been talk of a court case over the separation, which would have been very rare in the 1960s.

My confusion was interrupted by 'Auld Baldy', as he was known, or the Surveyor, to give him his official title. I couldn't believe that he had the nerve to appear.

'Sad business this, very sad.'

The awful part of the whole terrible trauma was that it could have been avoided. Well, it never should have started. Jim was twenty minutes late in the morning: in the official jargon he was 'cut out'. Auld Baldy had drawn a line at 9.15 a.m. and signed the attendance book. Jim had lumbered up the stairs, taken one look at the book and let out an unmerciful string of oaths.

He sat at his desk, ignored everyone in the room, glanced through the *Irish Times* but balked at the crossword and sulked until the tea break. He left without a word, heading for the local boozer, which was what he usually did even on a normal morning. My desk was immediately behind his and I recognised the pattern. 'Baldy' later knew that Jim was missing, and I was dispatched to find him.

Jim was still very angry, despite a few glasses of whiskey, at about half eleven when I told him that his absence had been observed. His response was predictable. He just carried on drinking and he never reappeared in the office. He drank with anyone that presented themselves. I looked for him when I finished work, but he had moved on.

'He's gone looking for grub.'

The barman seemed relieved.

Everyone knew the precise details the next morning as if they were present throughout the saga. Jim arrived in a city centre store and walked up the stairs to the restaurant, stopped suddenly at the top, clasped his chest and toppled over. He was dead by the time they got him to the hospital. He was not the most popular man in the office – many saw him as a contrary old bastard forever arguing the toss and creating problems. However, his sudden shocking death struck home very deeply among most of the staff.

I was inconsolable, but one of the lads put some perspective on it.

'Look, Frankie, he drank heavily every day – it was going to happen sooner or later; he was in his sixties, overweight. He was on quarterly reports so Auld Baldy was going to keep the pressure on; inevitably he was going to topple over.'

'That's bloody callous.'

'Yes, maybe, but nonetheless true: he spent all his life fighting and arguing; for God's sake, he was impossible. Look, when I was in Personnel branch there was a file that thick it would choke a sow. It is all very sad, boy, but that's the way it is. There will be very few upset by all this; maybe his daughter, but many will get half pissed and say he wasn't a bad auld skin, but that's the usual rubbish. Mourn him if you wish, but ...'

The voice trailed off. I didn't bother to tell him that after the funeral I had cried quietly because I liked Jim in spite of everything and I could see how alienated and lonely he had become without any apparent friend, official or personal.

He detested most women, probably because of his failed marriage, constantly trotting out what had almost become his signature tune: 'Sure they were all made for the one thing and most of them are no bloody good at it anyway.'

And then the big derisive laugh.

There was more, much more, and I often wondered where it all came from, but he rarely engaged with me on any real personal stuff. He was near enough to retirement, drinking alone most of the time except for a few auld strays that were equally adrift.

About a month after his death I was approached by one of his contemporaries and asked if Jim had ever mentioned anything about a will. None had been found, and someone said I might have an idea. That was probably the last time his name was mentioned. I wondered who would get his gratuity; it was a tidy enough sum.

About two years later I was promoted. Working in Excise, I went into a small bookmaker's office in Dublin. When I had finished my verification of the records the middle-aged lady clerk, friendly and good humoured, tried to enlist me in her struggle with the Crosaire crossword in the *Irish Times*. I was no help. She asked if had been at this work for long, and out of the blue asked if I knew Jim Byrne. Then she said: 'I was married to him for a good few years.'

My mind raced back to the day in the morgue, but I couldn't see any resemblance to the woman I saw there. I was tongue tied, but managed to stagger out a few words about being sad when Jim died, and then left.

Oddly, it was the fact that they both were practitioners of the Crosaire that stuck with me. They probably often did it together in the good days.

20

SERENDIPITY

New Year's Eve is one of those nights that I would gladly abolish. It excites this mad compulsion in many people to make it the most important social night of the year. It hardly requires description, but most venues are thronged with everyone pretending to be deliriously happy. It defies understanding. One is expected to turn on an instant gaiety at midnight and with joyous abandon hug almost everyone in sight. It is a totally different matter if one is among a few close friends, but the expectation that one must behave in a certain fashion because of some silly tradition has always given me some problems. It was no different back in 1962.

Tom, my friend, ably assisted by his girlfriend, decided that I needed a partner – that is, a female woman of the opposite sex. The thought of a 'blind date' was not immediately attractive, but I didn't have the heart to refuse when invited to Islandbridge Tennis Club. Having failed to wriggle out of it, I found myself being introduced to this girl in the club on New Year's night. She was nervous, trying her best to be friendly, and I did my best, but it was patently obvious to me that it was not a good match. We danced, but, to be honest, I didn't make the necessary effort. It was very embarrassing and I excused myself pretty quickly. In spite of much pleading and cajoling, I remained adamant. It was tricky, but I was left in no doubt that I should look for a different lift home. It did not promise well for the midnight celebration.

I hung about for a while and noticed this elegant lady across the hall wearing a light brown skirt and matching blouse; she had a scarf thrown nonchalantly around her shoulder. She was without any doubt the most attractive woman in the hall. She smiled when I asked her to dance. Polite chit-chat followed on the aftermath of Christmas, including Christmas cards, about which I had very strong feelings and an even stronger urge to express them. There was instant disagreement between us: we hardly lasted one set before taking leave of each other; a polite, cold 'cheerio'. It was extraordinary but it didn't leave either of us heartbroken.

The search for a lift home was the most immediate matter. In the aftermath of the midnight débâcle that greeted the New Year, I was smoking my pipe in the corner and I struck up a conversation with a small, lively and very talkative girl. It led to a lift and an invitation for tea in her flat in Rathmines. A few had gathered, but it was not exactly a lively affair – the Lady of the Christmas Cards was there, and in fact resided there. After cold tea and biscuits I found myself without much option but to start walking my tired frame back to Glasnevin.

Leinster Cricket Club in Rathmines was renowned for its Saturday night 'hops'. I became a regular, and discovered to my great joy that one of the staff in the Customs was the 'Head Lar' there. Mick loved to show his authority, but to his eternal credit he never made any compliment of letting me in free. (There was one famous night much later than this period when five of us turned up to find the 'full house' notice displayed. Mick did the trick, and we all waltzed in free.)

One Saturday night in 1963, who should I meet in the Leinster only the Christmas card lady from Islandbridge. She smiled again when I asked her to dance. We were more circumspect with each other, and there was a definite lack of contentious subjects. I have a very clear recollection of the occasion forty-five years later. She had a poise and a calmness about her which was rare in my experience of young women. There was no denying her beauty, but the effect was utterly different from the first encounter, which of course was affected by the fallout from the blind date débâcle. I discovered that she was a trainee midwife, having qualified as a nurse the previous year. From Galway, her family now lived in Thurles, so there at least the Tipperary connection. I suppose I was clutching at straws, narrowing it to that kind of minimal common background.

It ended with me walking her back to her flat, which was about a hundred yards away. After tea – warmer than the previous visit – and biscuits, I had the effrontery to ask her out. She agreed, but told me that she had a boyfriend in Derry, and as she was on shift work in the Coombe hospital her hours could change. The walk back to Glasnevin that night was a little sprightlier, and indeed I was delighted with my good fortune.

The following Saturday night I took Maree Fahey, the nurse from Galway, to the Palmerston Rugby Club dance in Milltown, which was seen as a little more upmarket than Leinster in the petty snobbery of the time. We had just emerged from our respective cloakrooms when there was an announcement by one of the band that there was a phone message for my ladyfriend for the night. She came back a lot less calm than I had seen her, but far from upset, and announced that the man from Derry had appeared in the flat unexpectedly.

It was my turn to be calm and collected. Always good at accepting the inevitable, without too much fuss we were in Eglinton Road hailing a taxi. That was the end of the affair for then.

The other side of my character emerged when I returned to the club with the 'pass-out' I was careful enough to gather on my way out. Hanging around for a while, my heart was not in it and I set off on a long, forlorn walk to Glasnevin once more.

21

TRANSFORMATION

At a glance, it is glass that dominates the Irish Financial Services Centre (IFSC). An informed architectural view might make a more critical assessment, but it is undeniable that these striking edifices make a startling contrast to the stately elegance of the Custom House on the sweep of Memorial Road. It is hard to know what the ordinary people of Dublin make of this mysterious place – maybe they are oblivious of the activities of the financial gnomes. Flashing screens manned by eager young professionals send millions of euros whirling around the corridors and out across the globe, while simultaneously enticing millions of dollars and various other currencies back into the system in some magical wizardry.

It is another intoxicating image of swirling spirits and wine, imported from many corners of the globe, that is embedded in my consciousness.

The IFSC was built on the warehousing site of the former Custom House Docks Board. A range of bonded warehouses operated there under the control of the Customs and Excise. Unimaginative names like Stack A, B Wet and B Tobacco housed thousands of gallons of spirits and wine in casks and cases. Huge quantities of tobacco also were stored there. The excise duty was hugely significant at the time, and the State depended then as it does now on this revenue to keep the auld ship afloat.

The warehousing system was simple: traders were allowed to import these high-duty goods and deposit them 'in bond' under the control of the Customs and Excise. The duty was deferred until the importers were ready to take delivery. It was an ideal system which facilitated the trade. All of this activity involved the keeping of a plethora of records, with an unimaginable number of calculations. There was one adding machine, which a junior like me never even got near. This regime contrasts starkly with the present armoury of technology with its illimitable range. It is another striking example of the way this country has been transformed. In the 1960s and 1970s there was a ten-foot-high wall of galvanized tin surrounding the site. It disappeared in the name of progress, like so much else that was a little more valuable.

Among a number of Excise officials who ran this Warehouse operation in the 1960s was a Cork man named Andy Desmond. He was the father of one Dermot Desmond, who conceived the idea of attracting the financial representatives of the world banking scene here. This idea just grabs my imagination in a way that is hard to convey. I don't think that the father took the son aside and whispered gently to him about the commercial possibilities of the site … but of course if he did it would have been quite legitimate, as the sale of the site was a regular open-market transaction. It is the influence of the father on the son that really interests me.

Andy, who has gone to his eternal reward, was a jolly character, a little overweight and often quietly referred to as 'the fat man'. His carefree attitude belied a steely ambition which was later realised. Promoted a few times, he became the senior official in the South East as Collector Customs & Excise Waterford. He spent his last official years in Dublin Castle, having come a long way from his humble beginnings as a uniformed Preventive officer.

The Customs and Excise service had more than its share of characters. The varied nature of the job and the necessity to labour alone in isolated locations led to some casualties, but also to the emergence of strong-minded, independent men who were fearless. It really was a joy to meet some of them when one did short periods of relief. They had an insatiable desire for news and gossip from those of us who were unattached and floated between different locations.

Paddy and Joe were a formidable combination when I worked in B Wet. Paddy was a Dubliner with a sharp intellect and an even sharper tongue. He spent his day talking and deliberating, but he was extremely touchy and one just had to humour him. Joe was totally different – an amiable soul, saying very little, but the occasional remark and the twinkling eyes behind the rimless spectacles conveyed more than a thousand words.

Paddy and Joe had two or three regular official callers at about 'fourish' on their way home. Spirits were regularly sampled for analysis to determine the appropriate duty rate; inevitably remnant samples were retained in the office as they could not be returned to the casks. A longstanding tradition allowed some of this gloriously mature liquid to be consumed on the premises. Paddy was like a senior cleric as he reposed behind a large desk and extracted all the gossip. Juniors like myself literally never even got a smell of the stuff, and were often gently moved to an outer office to facilitate the interaction.

There is a pub in the IFSC at the moment. This really made me smile when I made the discovery. It probably is the scene of many confidential exchanges with huge financial implications. Maybe it is a bit fanciful, but I feel that it is all small beer compared to what was exchanged in the old warehouses at the confidential sessions. One reflects on the Arms Crisis, as it was known, in the late 1960s and on the conspiracy trial in 1970, which involved the evidence of many Customs officials over a protracted period. My imagination runs into overdrive when I think of what may have been exchanged by these wise old officials in that very unusual period in the history of the State. Some of what took place has never been satisfactorily explained.

There was one fascinating story relating to the importation of arms, which was the subject of those court proceedings. It was never related in evidence, but one senior official received a telephone call from head office enquiring if he could trace an importation of 'mild steel cake' in his district. He failed to trace the consignment, but had many colleagues damned to know what it could be. The amusement was somewhat tempered when it was discovered that the real consignment of arms appeared on the manifest as mild steel plate. The raucous laughter from the inner room was often a clue that the old joke was being trotted out again.

It turned out not to be so funny in the end, like so much more that transpired during that tumultuous period, but Paddy and Joe and their contemporaries are all long past caring now, as sadly they have moved on to their eternal rewards.

22

THE OFFICIAL INTRODUCTION

'Well, kiddo – did the bird bring you down to meet her folks yet?'

'I'm still dodging it.'

'If you're interested I'm driving down on Friday week, no sweat for me to stop off in Thurles; course I'd pick you up on the way back – you'll hardly move in straight away.'

His mocking hyena laugh was his trademark. Tom made fun of almost everything; sacred or trivial would attract some form of derision. Occasionally he exploded in a tirade of obscenity without any real provocation. Colleagues trod lightly and gingerly around him. I found him easy enough to work with, and I took him as I found him. In his early forties, he was married with a family, about which he rarely spoke.

He had arrived unexpectedly in the FPP from the provinces, apparently on a compulsory transfer. The grapevine had not revealed the full story. 'Problems with the jar' was heard, but he didn't drink now and was destructively critical of the crew that drank during official hours. He smoked incessantly. 'Mood swings' was not a term much used in the early 1960s, but it aptly described Tom's behaviour.

The Galway Nurse worked in the Coombe Maternity Hospital. We got on well most of the time, and she had this almost imperceptible allure that I couldn't resist. That sounds just a little pretentious, but how can one adequately describe the indefinable?

The official trip to Thurles to meet Maree's parents had been mooted and, while I had agreed in principle, it had been left in abeyance. This offer of a lift seemed right at the time.

When Tom picked us up in an Austin Mini — they were hugely popular at the time — we were surprised to find that he had another passenger: a very serious looking girl with short blonde hair and glasses, about our own age.

'Yer wan lives down the road from me auld wan; I'm just giving her a lift home. A pauper like yerselves with no car, and it's not what you think Frankie.'

The girl — she was never introduced — remained impassive. She probably knew his form, but I wondered if she knew this was a hired car. A bike was Tom's normal mode of transport.

We reached Naas pretty quickly, Tom chattering gaily and undemandingly. The girls in the back were remarkably quiet. I was very surprised when he pulled over in the main street.

'Do you fancy a jar, kiddo?'

'Not really, Tom — I'm OK.'

'Ah come on — 'tis thirsty work. Right girls — all out.'

The small pub had two customers in a corner; they showed no interest in our arrival.

'My treat, kiddo, and by the way, forget about your offer of petrol money — I hope to make a good few quid out of this trip, so no messing, OK?'

My protests were ignored. The girls had orange juice and I had a glass of lager. As he paid for the drinks at the counter Tom had a glass of what looked like whiskey in his hand. He downed it in two slugs and when he returned he had a second glass. I said nothing, but my expression would have said it all. Maree was looking at me rather strangely.

'Well girls, what's the craic? How do you put up with this client, Maree? He's a right gobshite at work.'

The hyena laughter echoed in the small bar.

'Do you know I'd not fancy him coming home with my daughter if I was your auld fella?'

Maree laughed unconvincingly. The other girl kept her head bowed.

'One for the road, folks? Frankie?'

'No, Tom, I'm OK — what about heading on?'

'Shortly — don't worry, kiddo. Girls?'

Heads moved slowly, declining.

He demolished the whiskey at the bar. We were herded back into the Mini.

On a very uneven road surface, the less than perfect suspension in the Mini was severely tested. Tom was quiet, focused on the driving. Suffering from delayed shock and perplexed at his unexpected behaviour in the pub, I wasn't ready for another stop in Port Laoise. Silently I cursed my stupidity in getting trapped.

'You'll need a stiffener, kiddo, before you face the folks?'

'Tom, I'd rather head on.'

'We will in my arse – I need a quick one.'

I followed him in. The girls remained in the car. He was consistent; another whiskey, also large. A lager for me. He sensed my unease.

'Relax, Frankie – we'll be there in no time.'

'Didn't know you took a drink, Tom.'

'Only very rarely, but when I hit the main Cork road I let loose.'

Nodding, I looked into my glass.

'Don't start sulking on me now – we'll be fine.'

He spoke as if a drop had not passed his lips.

'Come on before someone runs away with the girls, not that anyone would take the yoke that I brought. Your wan is a fine bird.'

The journey to Thurles was uneventful but the level of tension in the car had risen significantly.

'Hope yer auld fellow takes a jar, Maree.'

It was clear he needed food, and Maree invited him in. Tom was out of the car and up the garden path before we had gathered our wits. Maree's mother opened the door and was confronted by a loud wailing guffaw.

'I'm your new son-in-law Mrs, give us a hug!'

The unfortunate woman didn't know what was happening. It was like a scene from a very weak farce. While Tom was ensconced in the bathroom, I was introduced to Maree's parents. It was probably one of the most unimpressive and embarrassing introductions imaginable.

The meal passed without incident or any alcohol, much to Tom's annoyance. Tom and his passenger left for Cork as Maree's mother threw holy water on the car.

It was a pleasant, uneventful two days, in spite of the earlier turmoil. I was uneasy about the return journey and considered returning by train. There was no way of contacting Tom, and I feared that it might be better to stick to the original arrangement. Sunday mid-morning after mass the unease reappeared. It was tossed about at lunchtime, but we did nothing; we were waiting quietly at sevenish when the doorbell rang.

A wild-eyed, dishevelled Tom bounded into the kitchen.

'How yee folks, all set to move, well what do ye think of this client for the daughter?'

Clearly Tom was moving on more than his own energy: almost out of the air like a magician he produced two 'Baby Powers' – clear, amber liquid. Maree's mother's sharp intake of breath was hard to ignore.

'Who'll join me to celebrate yer man?'

Maree's father said very simply but cogently: 'Not a good idea when you're driving – maybe you should leave that stuff till later. Put on the kettle, Mam.'

'Ah come on – don't be a spoilsport, boss.'

It went on like that for a while until Tom copped on. He was not allowed to drink in the house. I knew we were in trouble, and cursed my stupidity for not going on the train. It was too late now – we were stuck.

In a few minutes Maree's father, a quiet, inoffensive man, had prevailed on Tom to hand over the two measures.

'All right, you can have them – you'll need them being stuck with that auld wan.'

He had stepped over the acceptable mark. His remark hung in the silence momentarily and then his mawkish attempt at softening it failed.

He had tea and sandwiches and we decided to go with him. Maree was uneasy and I tried to fool myself into thinking that he was not really inebriated: maybe it would be all right.

The unnamed girl had not reappeared; as if reading my thoughts, Tom said: 'I threw her out on the way down – no one will miss her, don't worry.'

The expression on Maree's mother's face was priceless. She got out the holy water and we left as her lips began silently imploring her God.

Tom drove very fast once he hit the main road. He was silent and seemed very concentrated. He stopped approaching Port Laoise and picked up a hitch-hiker, a young soldier returning to the Curragh Camp. The lad was delighted. He was questioned about his weekend but he was reticent. Suddenly Tom began to drive furiously, as if pursued almost.

'Take it easy, Tom – we're in no rush.'

'I bloody am in one hell of a rush or the bloody pubs will be closed!'

After about ten minutes the young soldier asked to be let out – his voice betrayed his fear.

'You can shagging stay where you are now, the Curragh you said and the fucking Curragh it'll be.'

The speedometer needle climbed up beyond the 70 mph mark.

'Don't you start now!' he hissed.

The young soldier was very relieved as he scrambled out of the car on the edge of the Camp. I sat there and just prayed. The prayers were answered; we arrived safely.

He was gone in a flash, having dropped us at Maree's flat.

I didn't see him for a few weeks; his change of duties took him elsewhere. 'Are you still chasing that nurse?'

That was the only reference to the trip. He left the office shortly afterwards on a transfer. We met rarely after that. Anytime I remembered the trip, it gave me the shivers.

At least Maree's parents were left to enjoy the small 'Baby Powers' at their leisure. Their real feelings about the débâcle were not revealed, and they raised no objections – that I heard anyway – to our marriage the following year.

Which of You Is It?
(for Maree)

'Which of you is it?
The question hangs awkwardly
as I examine the floorboards.
My wife's hesitancy earns an
enveloping hug from a tall
warm hearted American lady
'You poor thing – they're great here'
her voice trails off as I wish
fervently to be very far away.

A tiny smiling nurse takes her
to weigh, measure and examine,
not forgetting to sample blood
and various other bodily fluids.

Reunited after her testing and
prodding we sit waiting. Aware
the dreaded Cancer word has yet
to be uttered; my troubled reverie
interrupted by the call into
the all-knowing presence.

Presumably

'Presumably your wife will get better,'
Unlocking my bike desperately fleeing
the well intended sympathiser.
Pushing into the oncoming traffic
His voice still grating in my skull.
Anxious to get home with my
explosive cocktail of tiny white pills
So much to be learned about silence.

23

ASSUMPTIONS

It was like driving over an endless series of bridges. There was a peculiar tacked-on aspect to what is called US1, the Overseas Highway. It strings the islands together from the end of mainland Florida to Key West, which is the most southerly point of the Continental United States.

We had left Palm Beach early in the morning, and I was a very comfortable passenger in my son David's huge and ancient limousine. Half dozing in the subtropical heat, I was barely aware of the exotic surroundings as we sped south: Islamorada, Key Largo, Grassy Key and Boca Chica Key. A sudden torrential shower cascading on to the windscreen made driving almost impossible, and reminded us we were in hurricane country.

On the outskirts of Key West we stopped at a tourist office and arranged accommodation. I just observed: this reversal of roles is great; maybe it's an acknowledgement of all the driving and booking that I managed over the years. The Old Quarter in the centre of Key West is a series of narrow one-way streets, all awash with colourful sweet-smelling vegetation. Open trolley cars trundled noisily along. Late September is seen as the beginning of the low season, but there was no shortage of tourists.

That first evening we decided to get into the tourist mode by cruising in the Gulf of Mexico, with enticements of free beer and spectacular views of the sun setting. Billed at $25 per skull, the beer seemed not quite free. We boarded a double-decker craft, well equipped and spacious enough for an assorted group of about fifty or sixty tourists. As we eased out into the Gulf, there was loud calypso music playing in the warm, gentle breeze. A signpost on the top deck said 'Cuba 80 miles'.

A young and cheerful crew dispensed the beer generously. On the second offering the waiter asked: 'Where are you guys from?'

'We're Irish,' I replied.

'Do you still live there?'

'My Dad still lives there but I live in Palm Beach,' David said.

The waiter half stopped filling my glass. I could feel the sudden jerky movement as he pulled back hastily and looked at us.

'You're father and son!' he exclaimed.

His expression of amazement, or maybe it was shock, startled me. He began to cover his reaction by telling us he was South African. Then he moved on quickly.

We both laughed, but said nothing for a while. It was clear and unmistakable from his reaction; the look said it all. He had assumed we were a gay couple. Initially I was surprised and then amused. I could see the funny side of it.

It was simple enough. A young guy with an elderly companion in a place that was described as having a swinging gay population. Who could blame him?

We were served by a different waiter for the rest of the voyage.

Later, back on terra firma we sauntered down Duvall Street in the Old Quarter, in search of a restaurant. David decided against several places with just a shake of his head. It seemed he was making assumptions now.

We talked about the incident over dinner: we could see how it had happened, but we reached no positive conclusions. David revealed that when he was booking the hotel room, he had been offered a double bed. He had decided not to tell me this at the time.

The following day we came upon Ernest Hemingway's old house, where he is reputed to have written *For Whom the Bell Tolls* and *The Sun Also Rises*. The former home of Harry Truman, the late President of the USA, was another place we visited. Sadly, a warning notice about pollution deterred us from swimming in the Gulf.

We moved on after three days, back up the beautiful straits to the mainland. We never did see the sun setting – in fact it never even appeared that evening – but we got within 80 miles of Cuba.

I suppose we also learned something about making assumptions – for a while at least.

24

A JOYFUL SERVICE

During regular visits to my son and his family in Boston I had become familiar with the suburb of Brighton. Overlooking the bus stop I frequently used was an Episcopalian church. The entrance was distinguished by large pillars on each side. A wooden notice board in the front garden proclaimed a Saturday evening service and an early Sunday morning one at 8 a.m. Almost discreetly at the bottom of the notice a further gathering was mentioned, at noon on Sundays. The building bore a marked similarity to the Presbyterian church in my home town of Clonmel. As I write, it occurs to me that I was never inside that building during my time in the town.

Getting off the bus one Saturday night, I was surprised by the joyful sound of rousing hymn singing. The people gathered at the entrance suggested a full house. Raising the rafters was the phrase that occurred to me as I reflected on the uplifting sounds of praise. I promised myself a visit before leaving Boston.

It was raining the following morning, and I didn't feel like a thirty-minute walk to the nearest Catholic Church. It seemed like a good time to fulfil my promise. The old Sufi refrain came to mind … There is no God but God …

Surprisingly, at 11.55 a.m. I found the church empty except for four young African-American girls who were playing around the pews. When I approached them and asked politely about the service, they stopped, stared and then ran off behind the altar. I had a funny feeling that I was being observed from somewhere. A clock chimed twelve and a group emerged from behind the altar. Five women, four young girls and a male preacher carrying a Bible. All were African-American.

My first reaction was that that this was a private prayer meeting. I was more than a bit taken aback. I had expected a large congregation into which I could have slipped quietly. While I was considering my position, even a quick departure, one of the women approached me in the middle of the church, smiled, welcomed me and invited me to join them at the front. I knew then I was in for the long haul.

They launched into rousing hymns accompanied by cymbals banging and Halleluiahs. The group seemed to gather energy with each hymn. The cymbals were being rattled with real feeling. A smiling elderly lady broke free from the group and shuffled or half waltzed around the church, singing her own litany of praise. There was a lovely easy rhythm to her movements, and she smiled all the time. She came over and put her arms around me and told me how much the Lord loved me. 'You gotta let Him love you Brother.'

I decided to go with the mood as best I could, but I was very conscious that while I felt an outsider, these people were making a huge effort to make me feel welcome.

It seemed we were standing for hours when the singing stopped and the preacher went to the pulpit. He began by welcoming me and said, 'There must be a reason why you are here Brother, and whatever it is you are welcome and we trust that you find what you are seeking.'

The old lady whispered to me that the preacher was married to her daughter, and that the other women were also her daughters 'but their husbands don't pray too much'. The sermon was on the theme of forgiveness and its essential place in the Christian life. It lasted a very long time but I managed to refrain from looking at my watch.

I was wilting after nearly two hours, and I was relieved when the service ended. There was much hugging at the end, especially from the old lady. I was invited back and it was clear that the invitations were genuine. Emerging into the afternoon sunshine I felt a warm glow of acceptance and I was delighted that I had stayed on. There was no doubt in my mind that I had been part of a genuine act of worship. Their effort to welcome the stranger was particularly significant. I knew that I was privileged to have been there.

My son Kevin was amazed later when I related my experience. There was mention of crossing the racial divide and that maybe I had been a little naïve. I suggested that he could ask the group on Tuesday, as I had invited them to call. His amazement turned to shocked horror until I told him I was only joking.

I have not revisited the church, but I sent the community a Christmas card and thanked them for their warmth and kindness to a struggling soul.

~ ~ ~

Bill Somers

Detective Superintendent Bill Somers was the successful chief Garda negotiator in a siege in Bawnboy, Co. Cavan in January 1997, when a man barricaded himself in a house with his mother, after a shooting incident during an eviction. He also negotiated the successful release of the kidnapped Jennifer Guinness and Don Tidey in dramatic and dangerous circumstances.

Bill had a distinguished career of over thirty-five years' service at all levels in the Garda Síochána, which was marked by his selection to escort many visiting notables including Pope John Paul II, Canadian Prime Minister Pierre Trudeau and President Bill Clinton.

He was a longstanding member of the Garda Rowing Club, with which he rowed for many years, and a member of the Irish team at the 1976 Montreal Olympics.

He was married to my sister Helen. Sadly, he died in June 2010.

Negotiations
(for Bill Somers)

Long haul from Portmagee to Bawnboy
via Clonmel. Over fifty years of family service.
All the distilled wisdom needed in fifty hours
of listening and talking and listening.

Your father's uniform would have exploded
with pride. Can you imagine him
telling his colleagues in Clonmel
about the youngest boy from William Street?

He stopped me once, no light on my bike.
Roughly packed me home.
A different job in a saner age.

You were taught a lot about waiting,
learned the hard lesson over the years,
in a kind of Southern silence
often seen as distant; but you waited.

What about the other story that
unfolded in the cauldron of Bawnboy?
A little known place that defines remote.
A long way from South Kerry.

25

FINISHING THE YEAR WITH A BANG

I saw the racquet turning in Eddie's hand but it didn't prevent him striking the ball with all the usual force, propelling it in my direction instead of onto the front wall. There was a muffled dull thud as the squash ball fitted neatly into my eye socket, causing a blinding flash of coloured shapes. The shattering shock just stuck me to the floor. Immovable. The clatter of my racquet hitting the wooden floor was followed by a short, eerie silence. Eddie's voice sounded panicky: 'Frank, are you all right?'

I don't remember what I said, if anything, but later on I muttered what became a refrain almost: 'I saw your racquet turning as you hit the ball.'

It was New Year's Eve 1974, about 5 p.m., in Mount Pleasant Squash Club in Ranelagh, Dublin 6, as I gazed into the large mirror to survey the damage. There was a patch of condensation on the mirror. When I rubbed it with my towel it did not disappear; I knew that was an ominous sign. I suggested that we should go to the Eye and Ear hospital, which was just a short distance away.

There was hardly anyone around. We were admitted to the doctor's room in the Outpatients Department very quickly. The eye felt very heavy with a throbbing sensation. The doctor, a young woman in her twenties, having established the circumstances of the injury spent a few minutes peering into both eyes. She made a telephone call, apparently to consult. I didn't hear a word, but I've never forgotten her opening remark as she turned around to face me: 'A massive haemorrhage at the back of your eye, we'll have to keep you in for observation, you will need complete bed rest in case of retinal detachment.'

She seemed under pressure and there was much sighing.

'Could I go home and tell my wife and come back later?'

This sounded daft and was treated accordingly. I was suffering from shock probably. I was put in a wheelchair and escorted to a ward; both eyes were bandaged and I was securely tucked up in bed. Eddie had volunteered to go and tell Maree the full story. He was less than happy. Understandably he was afraid of her reaction.

I lay on my back, trying to adjust to the total darkness and the alarmingly sudden realisation that I could be in very serious trouble. I had this recurring urge to lift the bandage to see if I had any sight left. I knew the consequences of a detached retina. The tone in which the information was conveyed increased my fear. There was a lot of noise in the adjacent wards – someone was singing and sounded half cut. New Year's Eve was developing. Maree appeared and steadied me just by her presence alone.

It was a long night. Fortunately I had taken the precaution of removing my pipe and tobacco before my clothes were taken away by the night nurse. I smoked my head off and it helped immeasurably, but I was still worried.

New Year's Day passed without incident. I was fed and I smoked and I slept. Maree called and left. Quiet and uneventful, apart from being moved to a semi-private ward where I was alone.

Just before lunch on the following day, a bright, cheerful young woman appeared, asked many questions about my circumstances and verified that I was covered by private insurance. As she gathered up her papers she asked politely, 'Can I do anything else for you?'

'Maybe you could tell me if doctors are employed in this hospital?'

A very long pause ensued. She was thinking very very hard.

'I'll have a word with the Ward Sister.'

She was gone in a flash. A nurse arrived and asked if I had a problem, but all I did was repeat the same question. I felt a little strange, as I could not see the lady. She expressed polite surprise – amusement, almost – and then I opened up. It was very simple – this was the middle of my third day in the hospital. Not a soul had even asked how I was feeling, let alone examined me. In quick succession the Ward Sister appeared and offered me Valium.

I declined, and the House Doctor was next in the procession. He talked about the need for complete rest, and left, but not before I unburdened myself again. It seemed they were awaiting the Consultant's instructions and were not prepared to make any move without his approval. He appeared shortly afterwards and apologised profusely, mentioning that no one had told him that I was there. I didn't react for once, even though I had serious doubts about his excuse.

He examined me for what seemed a very long time, peering into the back of both eyes. He prescribed complete bed rest to guard against a detached retina. The slow process of healing was explained, and that did nothing for my peace of mind. The healing could in itself cause scarring, but he was optimistic. I was really worried now.

Later that day I was persuaded by Maree to take the sedatives that I got faithfully every day of my sojourn.

I spent two weeks on my back. All my family appeared on a regular basis, as did some of my colleagues. The bandage was removed from one eye after about a week, and this made things more tolerable.

Paddy, a friend, brought me two 'Baby Powers' – glorious amber liquid, easily the best gift of my sojourn. He was chatting inconsequentially, and then just threw out the question: 'Suppose there will be a big compensation claim?'

I was taken aback, as Eddie – the man who had hit the errant ball – was on the other side of the bed.

'Ah, no point, Paddy – the Revenue Commissioners would take the most of it.'

Paddy's laugh suggested he was not convinced.

Paddy was remembered kindly on the following nights as I enjoyed a soothing glass of whiskey while puffing contentedly on the auld pipe. I was sharing the room with a gentle but nervous soul who was less than relaxed with my double addiction, and neither of us in full possession of our sight. I can still hear: 'Frank, for God's sake don't fall asleep with that pipe still going.'

Much later, after my discharge from hospital, another squash player – a solicitor – asked in a less than direct fashion if legal action was being considered. I was non-committal. It seemed he had been asked 'to sound me out'. It was never seriously considered – even though there was retinal scarring, my overall vision was not affected then.

In spite of that harrowing experience I played League squash from 1969 to 1977. It was a hugely enjoyable period. We won Division 3 of the Leinster League in 1973 and were runners up in Division 2 in 1975. Promoted to the Premier League, we struggled among players of a much higher standard – some interprovincials and internationals – but we survived, managing to win a few matches. I had the doubtful honour of playing Geraldine Barniville, the No. 1 ranked lady and the only one playing at that level. She cleaned me in straight sets for the loss of only five points, but complimented me in the return game, having done the same, on being the only player brave enough to turn up for a second game; the others sent subs. However, I have a clear recollection of the night in a crowded Fitzwilliam Club when presented with our Div. 3 decorative glass tankards after fourteen matches, and wondering 'was this all it was about?'.

Squash team, Leinster League Division 3 winners, 1977 (front: Michael O'Farrell, Joe Smyth, the author; back: Paul Smyth, Kerry O'Loughlin)

Now it is the more positive memories that are important. There was much social interaction in the Club and also at the many tournaments. I look back on the period with great warmth and gratitude. Those I played with were fine squash players, exceptional men really. It might not have happened if Johnie Hughes had not introduced me to squash and Tom Power had not lured me into membership of Mount Pleasant out of a semi-indolent period in the mid-1960s. Maree was the one who facilitated it all with her unqualified encouragement and endless patience. *Go mairfidh siad go deo.*

26

AN AWAKENING

Visits to Cistercian monasteries became a regular feature of my life from about 1971. The Cistercians live by the Rule of St Benedict, which emphasises hospitality; visitors of all creeds and none are welcomed with no obligations beyond the normal house rules. Always I found it a refreshing and reinvigorating break, both physically and spiritually, but gave up years ago trying to explain to others the reason I did it. I was blessed to meet some inspirational people, both lay and religious, over the years.

I cycled from Clonmel to Newcastle and over the Knockmealdown Mountains with my father in 1954, spending five days there. I did think about 'joining up' once, fleetingly, but by then I had discovered the allure of those mysterious creatures with long hair and longer dresses, and I knew where my calling lay.

In November 1992 I was in the monastery in Roscrea. As a pipe smoker I found myself among the 'addicts' congregating for the old puff. Having listened to a very boring and detailed account of a golf match, I withdrew to the sitting room feeling quite ragged.

'You're writing your memoirs I suppose?'

I groaned inwardly, putting away my notebook, but said to myself: 'Frank, be courteous to this man.'

'Sit down, Brother.'

'Ah no, I have a lot of things to do. You know I have a tape by Richard Rohr – did you ever hear of him? It is about the influence of strong women in our life' (Richard Rohr is a Franciscan priest based in Albuquerque, New Mexico, where he founded The Centre for Action and Contemplation – a well-known writer and preacher, but I was not aware of him then).

I muttered some reply and said I wouldn't mind listening to it, and then he was gone. This elderly monk's appearances and departures were truly remarkable, almost as if he were dropping in from outer space.

I went for a walk; when I came back the tape was on the floor outside my room.

That night I listened to it, and discovered that it was part of a series recorded at a retreat for a group of Sisters of Charity in Cincinnati. It was about celibacy and its place in the life of religious. It was interesting, but it was late and I actually fell asleep in the middle of it. Resolving to listen when I was more alert, I went to bed quite mystified as to why I was given the tape. The brother knew I was married with three grown-up children, even three grandchildren. Maybe I had missed something …

As part of a routine, five days was my normal stay and I would get up for the early morning Office at 4 a.m. on my last day in the monastery. When I awoke to the shrill sound of the alarm at 3.45 a.m. the cold winter darkness was just not inviting. I hesitated, remembered the tape and reached for my Walkman. I decided to try the other side of the tape. The rest of this story is hard to tell; at times words seem hopelessly inadequate.

A soft American voice introduced the topic as ' What God loves'; Richard Rohr briefly reviewed the previous week and said that he hoped that the Sisters had picked up the extent of God's love, and went on: 'The only free people are those who draw their lives from within, who know who they are and have been named by the Father and know that they have a soul. This week has been a journey into discovering that soul and to rejoice in it, but most of all to trust that soul and to know who you are before God. It is all that we have, and God is willing to make it for ever and no one can take that life away from you; you simply wait for that day when the Lord will say: "This life that you have, it is yours forever …"'

Rohr's voice then trailed off for a few moments, finishing with the final promise: 'That is all that we really have: all other things are passing away; all other things are various forms of illusions ... unearned life, unmerited love, unconditional life and love is the meaning of the Gospel and it is here right now and it cannot be achieved or accomplished, and some of you are going to believe that and you're home free; most of us kick and scream and will not believe the Good News and that finally is the only question, it is not if you are worthy of it but are you going to believe just like Mary did …'

Something began to happen very quickly. I can't describe it, but it seemed as if I was electrified – as I said, words are just not up to it. The intensity of what I felt is indescribable. I knew it was a special moment and I tried to savour it. I have never been so moved as on that night: I felt loved by God for the very first time in my life. I was aware of that love in a rather vague way, but actually realising it deep inside my being is hard to convey. I have wondered at the necessity to tell it publicly, and then I say 'why not?'. It is what I have craved all my life. As Rohr said in another context, quoting the mystic Hildegarde de Bingen: 'The veil had parted.'

The following day the Brother was a bit perplexed, but he was pleased for me. Looking back at the curious circumstances in which initially I didn't wish to engage with him and the way I sought 'the quiet place', it just left me astonished.

I gave copies of the tape to a few people – some did not respond and a few thought it interesting; one man who was looking forward to Rohr's visit here said he couldn't take the American accent and didn't listen.

The excerpts quoted above remain with me and continue to lift my spirit.

I went to hear Richard Rohr in Bath as part of a small group who had spent time in his Centre in New Mexico. Later, in 2005, I went down to New Mexico and spent a week in the Centre. It was a journey of thanksgiving. When I published a version of this chapter in *Spirituality* there was some small reaction, and Richard himself sent an email thanking me.

There is a great deal more on the tape, but one excerpt is worth quoting: Rohr talks about 'how patient God is with us and how He waits and He waits and lets us be, and then … one day when we least expect it, He reveals Himself.'

27

NODS AND WINKS

We met on Parnell Street in Dublin on a summer's afternoon about 1973. Paddy owned a shop in the vicinity and had gravitated there from a lifetime of selling as a commercial traveller. He was the President of the Conference of the St Vincent de Paul, to which I belonged. There was a weekly meeting on Sunday mornings, and between about twelve of us we visited five hospitals in the city.

'Ah Frank, there you are – working hard for the State I'd say.'

Followed by his nervous little laugh.

'As always, Paddy.'

'You don't hang about on Sunday morning – yourself and Tom do great work; we would be lost without ye.'

The little chuckle emerged again. I sensed there was something about to be dropped in.

'How would you feel about joining the Knights of Saint Columbanus?'

It was my turn to laugh. This was the very last thing that I could have expected, an invitation to the bloody Knights right in the middle of a busy street. Actually I laughed loudly and with great fervour. Paddy was taken aback.

'I'm serious, Frank: you do know about the Order I'm sure.'

As ever I jumped right in.

'What exactly do the Knights do?'

'Much the same as we do in the Conference, looking after the poor and less well off.'

'Ah I wouldn't have the time, Paddy, really I wouldn't. Sunday morning is getting a bit tricky at home as it is, honestly.'

There was a bit of a pause; he shifted about on the footpath and caught me by the elbow.

'You know your boss is a very prominent member?'

I can still recall my reaction. It was internal more than anything, but it took a real effort not to react.

'Who would he be, Paddy?'

He trotted out the name of the Chairman of the Revenue Commissioners.

'It wouldn't do your career any harm.'

I took a deep breath and then another. I was getting angry now – my tone changed.

'Not too sure about that, Paddy – no, not too sure at all,' then I made a conscious decision to lighten the mood.

'Did you ever read Mervyn Wall's novel *No Trophies Raise*?'

He thought I was mocking him, as reading would not be his forte. We parted on good terms, with Paddy exhorting me to discuss the matter with Tom.

After my session with Paddy his invitation had hung on my mind. I raised it with Tom on the following Sunday when we had finished in the hospital. He seemed more than a little amused.

'Sure nearly all the members in the Conference are also in the Knights. I thought you would have known that. Sure why are all our events, training and socials held in Ely House, the Headquarters of the Knights?'

His look of incredulity said it all.

'Why are you in it, Tom?'

He looked at me very sternly. I sensed his impatience.

'Well, firstly because I was asked, and secondly because it seemed a good idea to join at the time. The work is harmless … almost non–existent … huge mystique about it, and it is a secret society designed to combat Freemasonry, but that is a load of nonsense except they have a lot of members in select positions. [His voice trailed off as if he was unsure about continuing.] I know that I got jobs for each of my four sons. End of story. You will almost certainly get promoted if you join, as it is crammed with senior civil servants, but you probably have a conscientious objection to all that and before you start I don't wish to hear it. OK?'

I got the message. No more was said.

'Well, it sounds as if you should just go along and join them.' My good wife had no doubt even after listening to my long, tortuous but sincere objections. I believed it was totally unjustifiable to further the career of anyone on the basis of their membership of a Christian organisation and thereby exclude another person who might possibly be more suitable.

It opened up a huge Pandora's box as I looked back over my time in Revenue and reflected on the number of quite outrageous promotions against all the odds. Mervyn Wall's novel was set partly in the Civil Service and it showed the way the Knights operated in promoting their members, often excluding more deserving applicants. Many of the characters in the novel were shown to be degenerates who were also loyal Knights. There was a subtle menace tinged with humour running through the narrative. I can still recall my sister Helen laughing uproariously as she read the novel when we shared a flat in Drumcondra.

I spoke quite openly about declining the invitation among colleagues, one of whom remarked that I had told him that I had declined to join Opus Dei as well – which was true.

'You're not destined for the top in this job, Frankie.'

I never regretted my decisions.

The recruitment to the Knights of Saint Columbanus still goes on. Some of the secrecy at least is gone: there is a website which gives the Officers, a Mission Statement and other information. Women have yet to be recruited, which is not surprising. Also there are serious unanswered ethical questions about the organisation and the machinations of the members.

28

QUIET DAYS AT THE OFFICE

Tim was restless. His desk was directly in front of mine, and I couldn't fail to notice that he was moving around all morning. He sat between two very senior Customs officers, and his task as a Post Office clerk was simply to record the details of both their transactions. He was a quiet, thoughtful if rather serious man in his late thirties, but not totally devoid of humour.

Leaning across my desk, his face was too close to mine.

'Frank, do you know what I was thinking?'

I waited and moved back a little from his large, intense face.

'That seizure is most unusual – the sheer quantity alone, I can't figure it.'

His voice trailed off as he continued to gaze at me in what seemed like wonder, but I didn't really see it coming …

'Do you know, Frank, a dozen or two wouldn't be missed?'

I sat bolt upright, surprised – almost alarmed. I could feel the anger beginning to rise.

'What the hell are you talking about? Are you suggesting we should have a raffle or what – maybe announce an auction?'

'Ah hold on, will you boy? I'm not saying anything except it's a great opportunity.'

'Dream on, Tim, but not at my expense.'

I got up and walked away just to cool down. It was an outrageous suggestion and he knew it. To alter an official document and steal the contents would be unpardonable officially: almost certainly a sackable offence. To be known as the guy who stole the 'French letters' would be a fate almost worse than death.

One hundred and forty-four dozen condoms in an unmarked parcel going to what seemed a private address in the midlands was almost beyond belief. Occasional seizures of a half dozen condoms or so would go almost unnoticed unless there was an angry response from the importer commenting on the outdated regulations, particularly as the Criminal Law Amendment Act of 1936 applied.

'I just hopped the ball; I knew you wouldn't consider it.'

I left it at that. About three weeks later an official receipt came from Dublin Castle – the familiar envelope with meticulously neat and tiny handwriting was instantly recognisable.

'Mr Ó Marascail, Please note 144 dozen condoms advised, 145 dozen received. Please note the appropriate records.'

I just couldn't believe it; all I could do was smile. The initial count was clearly incorrect and no one had bothered to check it.

Would I tell Tim? I didn't really have any option, as he needed to alter his records.

I just put the receipt on his desk. He picked it up read it. He said not a word – I heard a sound like a sigh. He shook his head slowly and deliberately, handing it back. I could guess what he was thinking, but there was no point in provoking him.

Then unexpectedly in 1967 I was promoted after an interview – no matter how well one did, there were very few promotions from the FPP – leaving behind the drudgery and confinement of an indoor clerical job. After some intensive training and armed with a Commission from the State I found myself working in the rarefied world of Distillation and Brewing in the premises of Irish Distillers and Guinness. It was a rewarding, challenging job, collecting literally millions of pounds every month. A sobering experience to be reminded how much the State depended on the revenue derived from the legalised drugs of alcohol and tobacco.

It was towards the end of 1968, which had been a hugely significant year. Our younger son David had been born just sixteen months after his brother Kevin. It was also the year of the publication of *Humanae Vitae*, the Papal Encyclical of Paul VI, which decreed that only natural methods of family planning were permissible. It was widely believed that the committee appointed by the Pope had recommended a change that would have allowed the use of artificial contraceptives by married couples. The expectations of innumerable loyal Catholics were dashed. It left an ineradicable mark on the attitude of so many, and the results are clearly evident to this day in the huge decline in the number of practising Catholics.

Much of the world was in political turmoil also, with student riots in Europe, the racial disturbances in the USA and the awful misery in Vietnam. Our own island was hovering on the brink of civil strife. In the midst of all this social change the ordinary people were trying to live out their life as best they could.

I was placed on temporary reassignment to the Customs and Excise Letter Packet section in Parnell Square, where an older colleague, Tom, was genuinely surprised to see me and mad for any official news of a world that had apparently passed him by.

'Maybe they thought you needed a bit of humility boyo?'

As he spoke, the bell in the public office rang.

'Sure maybe you might try out some of that new fancy skill?'

As I walked out into a small private space, a counter separated me from two well-dressed, pleasant-looking women who were maybe in their late thirties.

'I got this in the post – can you tell me what it's about?'

It was the usual detention notice for undeclared letter packets. Having explained the legal situation, I left them briefly to get the packet. As I opened the outer wrapping I could sense their eager anticipation. As I discarded the outer wrapping the penny began to drop, and then I could see the familiar-shaped internal packets. Alarm bells began to sound in my skull. This might be very difficult – even confrontational.

As I placed the few internal packets on the counter, the woman who had produced the notice swore with great feeling.

'Who could have sent those yokes?'

The question echoed in the small space. She seemed quite genuinely shocked and embarrassed. Her companion was also uneasy and didn't know where to look. I tried unsuccessfully to soften the official tone: 'The importation of contraceptives is prohibited under the Criminal Law Amendment Act 1936 and the items will be confiscated.'

Their embarrassment was unaffected by my reassurance that there would be no further consequences to the seizure, judging by the blank stares directed at me. The awkward silence continued for a few moments until the second woman forcefully said: 'OK, let's go.' They almost rushed out in the end.

It seemed pretty clear that the woman was more than surprised and appalled by the experience. I believed that her reaction was not feigned. She would hardly have brought her companion if she had known. Of course I should have had the foresight to open the packet in her presence alone, but that might have brought its own complications.

I wondered later what the real story was – who had sent the condoms and what consequences, if any, had transpired at home.

Imagine the conversation or the lack of it as they walked down Parnell Square: and then maybe I misread the situation completely.

These events resurface almost every time I visit a chemist's shop. Conspicuously displayed, brightly coloured packets of condoms with alluring titles like Fetherlite, Ribbed, Gossamer and Extra Safe sit on many counters. Quite a change from the 1960s, but remember it was almost a quarter of a century later, in 1992, before legislation was introduced allowing the general sale of condoms. The 1979 legislation permitted their sale to married couples only.

Next time you see the display, spare a thought for those two unfortunate women and indeed for the generation that was subjected to such official foolishness.

The work, which was so varied and challenging, was a great leveller. It was all very well to be collecting millions from institutions, but constantly one was reminded of the realities of life and the need for humility and tolerance. Some of us required the regular reminders.

29

A PRISON VISIT

'I couldn't take my eyes off the photo: it was up on the cell wall, so I just spent most of the night gazing at it and looking at the stuff you wrote about the guys.'

This was the response of Frank Johnson from Swaleside prison in the UK. I had sent a Confirmation group photograph in which we both appeared, taken in 1950 in Clonmel. I had included details in so far as I could of the 33 other eager-faced boys. Nine were still living in Clonmel; the majority of the rest were in the UK.

An article by the novelist Joseph O'Connor in the *Sunday Tribune* in 1993 had highlighted the plight of the many Irish men imprisoned in English jails at that time. It focused on the case of Frank Johnson, who was convicted of the murder of John Sheridan, for whom he worked in a small shop in Whitechapel in East London. He was present in the shop when Sheridan was subjected to a petrol bomb attack by two men whose uncorroborated evidence implicated Johnson. Sheridan made a statement to the police exonerating Johnson, claiming that he had helped to quench the flames on the night. This statement was not produced at the trial of Johnson, who was not arrested until almost a year after Sheridan's death. Frank Johnson was sentenced to life imprisonment without leave to appeal.

Johnson dismissed his legal team during the trial and later told a graphic story of attempting to review his own case in semi-darkness in his cell. He did not go beyond primary school, and the mind boggles at this image of him trying to absorb legal documents.

Johnson had consistently claimed his innocence, and had impressed Billy Power of the Birmingham Six when they met during Power's fourteen-year term in jail. Unlike many prisoners who protest their innocence for the first few years in jail, but with the prospect of a parole hearing drop these claims, Johnson never relented; he showed no contrition and consequently was never eligible for parole.

A lengthy phone conversation with Andy Parr of the National Council for Civil Liberties in London led to my enlistment in the 'Campaign to free Frank Johnson'. Parr asked me some searching questions before he accepted that my interest was genuine. He saw me as an 'establishment' figure with my background in Revenue, and that it could affect my career. This amused me, but I understood it.

An interminable period of letter writing followed by lengthy silences became the pattern. Some of the politicians did reply, if in mainly vague terms. There was much sympathy for the plight of the unfortunate prisoner, but as he was incarcerated in the UK, little could be expected from Irish representatives except to keep the matter alive. Eamonn Wynne, a staff journalist on the *Nationalist* newspaper in Clonmel, campaigned unceasingly and compassionately, reporting any development in the campaign. He encouraged me and was instrumental in the publication of a number of my poems about Johnson and the campaign.

Frank and myself had a regular correspondence. It was remarkable how cheerful and hopeful he appeared – on paper at least – ending all missives with 'Be Happy'. He had regular visits from politicians and activists. The solid caring core was mainly on 'the left' in the UK, and was extremely active. I wrote to the Home Office and received a detailed outline of the case from C3 section, but as there was 'no new evidence' there was no prospect of an appeal. A letter to Tony Blair, then the leader of the Opposition, elicited a two-lined reply: 'I am just writing to let you know that I will consider what you have to say in your letter.' He never did let me know the result of his considerations.

However, some tangible evidence of positive responses emerged. An interview with Andy Parr by Sean Keane of the *Kilkenny People* resulted in a number of supportive letters arriving in Swaleside, including a few from the USA.

The Mayor of Clonmel, Seamus Healy, visited Johnson in Swaleside and created quite a stir when he arrived wearing his chain of office. This was one of the high points of the campaign. When Gareth Peirce, the distinguished lawyer, took on the case, hopes of movement towards an appeal began to rise. Her indefatigable work on behalf of the Guildford Four and the Birmingham Six had been crucial in their successful appeals.

All of this was heralded in the papers of 'the left' in the UK; however, there was no such bell-ringing in January 1995 when I arrived in North London on my way to Swaleside. On a Saturday morning, sitting in the back of Billy Power's tiny Fiat, hurtling down the M26 at 70 mph in torrential rain and very poor visibility, I wondered about my chances of making it back to Kilkenny safely. Billy's talking incessantly and passionately, giving the odd glance backwards to emphasise a point, was less than reassuring. Parr sat silently in the passenger seat, apparently unmoved.

The situation in the prison was a revelation. Most of the visitors were black women with many small children trailing after them. We were fingerprinted, photographed and given an identity card. No one actually looked at us or acknowledged that we were even present. It was eerie, with much pointing of fingers directing us as we were herded around. Going through a very long corridor with much unlocking and relocking of doors was a novelty for me, but I vividly recall wondering about the effect on a prisoner starting a sentence.

We were led into a large area not unlike a canteen in any institution. Small tables with four chairs; a coffee dock in the corner where sandwiches and snacks were on sale. There was a dais at the end of the room on which warders sat with that bored official look. Many cameras were strategically peering from on high. Then the prisoners began to appear. Mostly young black men looking anxious, but some came to life when they were greeted by their visitors. Frank Johnson surprised me. He was tall, slim and fit-looking with longish grey hair – almost distinguished looking. He was initially subdued; Andy Parr and Billy Power made a great fuss of him. He shook hands with me and thanked me for coming.

Johnson became very angry about the way in which a function to publicise his case had been mishandled, and he laid it all on the two visitors. It was very heavy stuff, and the angry sentiments just poured out of him. I was amazed at their meekness. Eventually I suggested as mildly as I could that these men were the pillars of his campaign and were indispensable. My intervention was ignored. I turned my interest elsewhere: at the next table a young black couple were intertwined in each other. An auld phrase from my youth, 'he was bet into her', came to mind.

I headed off in search of refreshments. Acquiring two pots of weak tea and some sandwiches actually broke up the angry debate. Billy Power tried to involve me by asking Frank what he recalled about his school days. 'He was up in the front seat, always a teacher's pet.' It didn't lead to any real discussion. One teacher was mentioned, as he had been in our letters; a particularly brutal one who went too far at times. It was pretty obvious that Frank Johnson was not really interested in the Irish campaign, and he made no mention of it. Some photographs that I had taken of a changed Clonmel captured his interest, particularly one of his own terrace. I had taken a shot of the town from the Comeragh Mountains and had it framed, but the understandable official response was that it could not be given to the prisoner as it contained glass. It was left in Swaleside: who knows where it ended up finally?

Billy Power of the Birmingham Six (left) and the author

Frank Johnson just stood there as we left. Forlorn. I felt very sad for him, having watched him at school, the punishment there, the emigration and now his life blighted by this injustice. Words are so inadequate. I wrote a poem which appeared in the *Nationalist* but … just words. The black couple had to be literally disentangled and they were the last to leave.

I couldn't find my ID card. A warder told me that none of us would be leaving until I found it. My grinning response was not appreciated. I found it after much fustering. It was a quiet journey back to Billy Power's house, where his very cheerful lady wife fed us all. Gareth Peirce was telephoned and given a detailed account of the visit, and that was it.

The campaign continued but Andy Parr was dismissed by Frank. I wrote to Frank for a while, and then I just ran out of steam over the years. When he was released in 2002 I wrote to him to mark the occasion. He had served 26 years.

He was deeply troubled that the Appeal Judge said the conviction could not stand as Frank was of unsound mind at the time of the trial. This was seen as a further injustice. It was believed by many in the campaign that a deal was struck to avoid a full hearing of an appeal, which excluded any consideration of the discovery of the witness statement by Mr Sheridan that exonerated Johnson. It ended as it had begun. He did receive some compensation eventually. By then the case was irredeemable.

His life outside was not great. The Power family looked after him until he got a small house, but the adjustment after the lengthy incarceration was too much. Frank Johnson died in November 2008, aged 72. He did not make it back to Clonmel before he died.

The author behind bar as an extra in Circle of Friends filming, 1995

30

NO SMOKING IN THE HOUSE, GRANDAD

Whenever I open my filing cabinet I am confronted by a large, voluminous file marked 'Donnelly Visas'. In the past it resurrected some very unsettling memories.

In the late 1980s and early 1990s thousands of Irish people emigrated to the USA under a quota system introduced after much lobbying by US Democratic Congressman Brian Donnelly and a few of his colleagues, including Senator Edward Kennedy. There is little doubt that the famous Green Cards opened up unlimited possibilities for many who would otherwise have been consigned to the humiliation of the dole queue.

The outbreak of the Gulf War in 1991 raised some serious issues for the holders of the Green Cards when it was revealed that there was a possibility of being drafted into the US forces; what had seemed a harmless paragraph now loomed as a stark reality. It is unclear just how many were aware that they could end up in the Middle East opposing the forces of Saddam Hussein.

My two sons were working happily in New Jersey when the awful truth dawned. The phone lines were buzzing across the Atlantic for a few weeks. I will never forget the night of 21 January when I heard a newscaster announce that Mr Bush had authorised the calling up of a further 20,000 into the armed forces. I was unable to sleep, and at 4 a.m. I sat downstairs smoking my pipe, wondering what was going to develop. It happened that I had just enlisted in a poetry group, so I tried to commit my troubled thoughts to a blank page. Eventually this emerged as part of the first poem I published ('Land of Opportunity').

The crisis passed. The lads were not drafted and went on to become naturalised US citizens. Over the following decades I travelled over to visit them on seventeen separate occasions. Once I had cleared US Immigration at Shannon I treated myself to a glass of Irish whiskey to set me afloat across the Atlantic. It always seemed the right thing to do.

Family photo: 'Celebration', 25th anniversary of Donnelly Visas, as shown on RTE in 2010

The first year that Kevin was installed in his own home I had negotiated a smoking room for my odoriferous pipe. The following year, when I assumed the same arrangement would apply, he told me that as his wife Deirdre was pregnant it would not be possible for me to smoke in the house. His manner was very apologetic and he seemed quite embarrassed. I can still remember his expression and the concern it revealed. This was a moment of some significance. The boy had become a man and the father had become ... well, not an errant child, but he was taking the directions.

Kevin came outdoors with me. It was a warm, balmy September evening in Boston and it turned into a pleasant interlude in the fading light, once the initial embarrassment had softened. Our relationship had always been special but had undergone a perceptible transformation once he was married.

'For this reason a man shall leave his father and mother and cling to his wife.'

On subsequent visits I settled happily on a bench in the garden and smoked quite contently. There was an apartment block visible from my position, and my imagination was given plenty of scope as the tenants moved about. There was even a group on the top storey who clearly gathered to smoke.

There is a change of location now. Kevin and Deirdre and three lovely grandchildren have come back home, relocating to Greystones. Boston is no longer on the map, and smoking is less attractive outdoors in this climate. I stick with my addiction. [1] However, there has been one unexpected development in that Heather, my granddaughter, is not too fussed on my pipe. The refrain of 'No smoking in the house, Granddad' is often heard in an imperious voice, followed by her screeching, mocking laughter. Even on the phone she scolds me, but the laugh raises my heart like nothing has ever done before.

A non-smoker would never have heard that beautiful, lifting, mocking sound of joy.

On Thanksgiving night in September 2011 the Dublin branch of Democrats Abroad honoured Congressman Brian Donnelly to mark the 25th anniversary of the introduction of the visas. The five of us were filmed among a large gathering of returned emigrants and their families in a Dublin hotel by RTE. Kevin and David gave a very brief account of their time in the USA. The cameraman, suggesting the untouched pint of beer on the table looked very lonely, asked me to take a slug. It was the last item on the 9 o'clock news that night. It did little for my reputation, but really it was about the celebration of the collective achievements in the USA by the recipients of the Donnelly visas.

Land of Opportunity

Mister Tree they called him.
A joke but the humour is lost
As the Tree grows into a Bush
Reductionism gone mad. Power.
War.
The Bush signed an order
Doubling the number to be
Drafted.
Almost missed in the welter of words.
That news is only important to some
Two Donnelly visas equals two sons,
Equals two US Marines.
Master's degrees and Leaving Certs
Excellent weapons designed
To kill.
Many more degrees on the other side
But they are used to suffering.
Mister Bush may allow them come home
To a neutral place run by Irish Midgets.

---

[1] This was correct when this chapter was first published, in an anthology. I did stop smoking, as described in a later chapter.

31

EVENINGS WITH
NORMAN MAILER AND E.L. DOCTOROW

'Thank you for the polite New England welcome – I knew I could expect it.'

Norman Mailer was right, as he faced about 1500 people who had thronged The Harvard Club on Commonwealth Avenue in Boston in 1991. There was no chairman, and Mailer was introduced by an unidentified man who announced that the writer would not be signing any books, even though his recently published novel *Harlot's Ghost* was on sale.

A small, broad-shouldered man with a shock of greying hair, casually dressed, he had a strong stage presence. Without notes or script there was a confrontational attitude about him, and one could sense that he was intent on 'stirring it up'.

Harlot's Ghost had received very mixed reviews. It depicts the political intrigue within the CIA in the 1950s and 1960s. A long, rambling book of over 1300 pages and many characters, it is enlivened by the unusual but highly imaginative portrayal of the interaction between the fictionalised John F. Kennedy, Frank Sinatra and Marilyn Monroe. It was totally different from his first novel, *The Naked and the Dead*, a savagely rough saga of the Second World War in South East Asia which had been a huge success in the early 1950s, catapulting Mailer into the limelight. He had lived most of his life in the public arena in the meantime. Married six times with nine children, Mailer had been living with his sixth wife, Norris Church, since 1980.

At that time he had published over forty books, and reams of journalism and political commentary. Mailer won the Pulitzer Prize twice as well as the National Book Award. Novels such as *The Executioner's Song* and *The American*

Dream as well as biographies including *Marilyn*, a life of Marilyn Monroe, had maintained a constant controversial profile. He was a co-founder of the *Village Voice* in Greenwich Village. The American public seemed to be divided in their opinion of him. His demeanour in public over the years had left a lot to be desired, particularly during the Vietnam War protests. He had moderated his behaviour somewhat, now sixty-seven but still always seeking the limelight.

On the night, Mailer was destructively critical of the political system and he did not spare either the Republicans or the Democrats. The ferocity of his remarks provoked several challenges and interruptions. Asked why he had never run for political office himself, he said that he had contested the Mayoralty of New York unsuccessfully in the 1960s. A convicted felon now, he was barred from holding office. At one stage he claimed that the Democratic Party had been infiltrated by the Republican Party. This enraged a section of the audience.

The writer's views on the growth of the Feminist Movement proved to be the most contentious part of the evening. It appeared that he was deliberately setting out to provoke the women in the audience. It was amazing to see him stand there, alone on the stage, apparently totally indifferent to the views and feelings of his audience. Many women left the auditorium in a noisy and angry way, while others just walked out quietly. The tone of these comments was summed up by his angry question to women: 'Do ya not know that ya can't do without us men?'

In the end people seemed to get tired of it all; the proceedings appeared to stammer to a halt. It was not surprising that there was hardly any applause at the end. A small crowd gathered around the author when he had finished. It was a peaceful group, and I ambled up. It thinned out with just one lady ahead of me, and I could hear their friendly interchange as she politely declined his invitation to join his group for dinner. Then suddenly I was facing the man himself.

I shook hands with Mailer and commented on his remarkable performance. He laughed heartily. I asked him what it was like working on one novel for seven years.

'Oh I took a break and directed a movie. It's just like a marriage where you can take a break and come back when you are refreshed.'

He was very relaxed and showed no strain after facing the hostile audience. I wished him well, and that was it. It was very hard to reconcile the earlier provocative behaviour with this friendly, charming man.

As I turned away my son Kevin appeared with a camera. It was too late: the moment had passed.

The following evening we ended up in Harvard at a talk by E. L. Doctorow, the distinguished author of many novels including *Ragtime*, *Billy Bathgate* and *The Book of Daniel*. It was less than memorable, but the Dean offered a glass of wine in his study to the audience. Never having darkened a Dean's study, it was hard to refuse. Maree trooped over not as enthusiastically as me, but it was a very pleasant evening and I had a few words with Doctorow, who told me he had received an award from Trinity College in Dublin. A very shy man, but the Dean was the opposite. This would not merit inclusion except that I discovered many years later that Doctorow had acted as an agent for Norman Mailer for a number of years before he published his own work.

I doubt if he would have said much about Mailer, but it was interesting to reflect on how easily I met two celebrated writers on successive nights, not to mention the Dean of Harvard who stocked some beautiful wine.

Mailer was interviewed on BBC TV by the novelist Martin Amis some years before his death in 2007. When asked at the end of the interview if he had any fears at that stage of his life, there was quite a perceptible pause during which he gazed beyond the interviewer. 'Decrepitude' was his answer.

32

THE MAN WHO INVENTED THE PILL

It was 2005; the lecture theatre in Trinity College was about half full. A middle-aged audience, more men than women. It seemed that many of the people knew each other. An air of expectancy was discernible.

A member of the Physics Department welcomed the Austrian Ambassador and thanked him for sponsoring the event, and then spoke briefly but glowingly of the guest speaker Carl Djerassi, who was a low-sized, very slim man with a neatly trimmed beard. He was clearly energetic – every movement suggested alertness, and he did not look like a man in his eighties.

His voice had an authority – his accent was not quite American, yet hard to pin down. This became clear when he spoke about his early years in Vienna, where both his parents were medical doctors. Movingly he described escaping the Hitler regime and landing in America with his mother. They had $20 between them.

It was very difficult to gain admission to a university. There was a suggestion of really just not knowing the way of things. He learned the ropes rather quickly, acquiring a PhD in chemistry at twenty-two and joining the Chemistry faculty in Stanford University. Djerassi made light of his scholastic achievements, but there was no avoiding his distinguished role as leader of the research team that synthesised the first oral contraceptive. Carl Djerassi was the man who invented 'the Pill'. He described in some detail how the various difficulties surfaced in the academic research and how it all finally came together.

The emergence of the contraceptive Pill in the 1960s separated sexual intercourse from procreation irreversibly. The social consequences were immeasurable, and unimaginable then.

His audience was riveted. Suddenly there was an interruption. A well-dressed lady stood up and said that she objected to his presence in the college. He listened to the first salvo and then said clearly: 'You are not going to interrupt my lecture – there will be time for questions at the end and you can make your contribution then.'

As the lady moved from her seat she paused and said loudly: 'I am leaving as a protest on the basis of my religious beliefs.'

It was hard to gauge the precise effect of the protest. It clearly interrupted his flow and it seemed to take the energy out of the presentation.

Djerassi spoke about his writing, the production of six novels and several plays which allowed him to educate and entertain a broader audience about scientific subjects in non-technical language. The exploration of the writing enlivened him again. His energy was remarkable. By simple arithmetic I reminded myself that this man was eighty-two, rising at 4 a.m. and starting every day with a half hour on a jogging machine.

The lecture finished fairly quickly. There was no time allowed for questions, but we were told that Djerassi's play *Calculus* was being performed in the Physics Theatre at 8 p.m.

As we left the lecture hall we were given a complimentary copy of his autobiography, *This Man's Pill*. There was a glass of wine on offer. As I stood on my own watching Djerassi surrounded by admirers, a man came over to me: 'Have you met this man at all?'

He sounded Irish and he told me Carl was his uncle. Before I could say a word he steered me into the presence of Djerassi.

Overawed, I made a few complimentary remarks about his lecture. His response was instantaneous: 'You must come to my play this evening.'

When I told him that I had to catch a train he was impressed that I had travelled to hear him. I had no choice but to accept. His genuine warmth really touched me.

When his nephew Paul handed him my copy of the book to be autographed, Carl thought the autograph was for Paul. There was a very funny interchange, with the great man slightly embarrassed at having signed a name known only within the family.

Calculus was given a dramatic reading exploring an allegation of plagiarism against the scientist Isaac Newton. A distinguished cast included Kate O'Toole and Bill Golding.

It was a remarkable night; my friends Jimmy and Joan O'Halloran stayed up until I arrived quite late. Amazingly, the unravelling of the night's events revealed that Jimmy knew the Djerassi family quite well in Ranelagh over the years. It seemed Paul's father had landed in Dublin when he escaped the Nazi regime. It was hard not to speculate about what might have happened if Carl had landed in Dublin also – or maybe what might not have happened.

Reminders

A mound of empty worn shoes
gaping starkly from a shiny postcard.
Innumerable, like their murdered owners.
Reminders of Vad Yashim visit.

Whisked around the horror chamber.
Spared no detail. Black and white
photographs reflect our numbed shock.
A woman leaves abruptly overcome with sadness.

The survivors lived with their memories.
We will replace ours within days,
with countless trivial tortures of our own.
No one spoke as we left.

33

THE WRONG SHOP?

When I enlisted in a course on African-American literature I did not realise that I would be the only man in a group with eight African-American ladies, mostly of indeterminate age. Africa Fine, who had just published her second novel, was a very welcoming group leader.

On the first Saturday morning, propelled by a gentle, warm breeze, I cycled the four miles to the West Palm Beach Library along a cycle lane, which was perfectly placed between the clear blue Atlantic and an almost deserted Intercoastal Highway. This library is unquestionably one of the most attractive I have come across: a haven of air-conditioned calm, where the large, wide windows overlook the Atlantic through the ubiquitous palm trees.

It turned out to be a lively but relaxed session. All the participants were more than familiar with the work of Toni Morrison, about which I learned quite a bit. As we finished up that first morning, Africa Fine invited the entire group to the annual Community Writers day on the following Saturday in Boynton Beach, about twenty miles further down the coast,

The reception area in the Community School in Boynton Beach was thronged with people of all shapes and sizes and from almost every age bracket. Everyone seemed in good humour, with the notable exception of two harassed clerks who were enrolling the participants in the various events. It was simply an open day embracing a range of the activities for adults in the local community school, including creative writing.

It did cross my mind that I might very well be in the wrong shop, as I was the only white person in sight. I considered withdrawing. My daughter-in-law, Dondra, who had driven me down, had suggested that the gathering might be 'a little ethnicky' and offered to come in and help me with registration. Her offer was declined with something a little less than gratitude. Then I reminded her that I had been invited. Maybe I was the only one who was aware of difference.

I hung in and, having registered for the princely sum of $5, found myself in a group of writers with six ladies, and a man who got the proceedings off to an acrimonious start by complaining bitterly that the local bookshop had not stocked his book. His complaints were duly ignored, and the chairperson focused on me, asking how I had discovered the event. The library group and Africa Fine gave me some credibility, but I felt that my expressed interest in writing for radio did not set the group alight. They listened politely, but their interest was clearly centred on the difficulties of being published, not unlike any similar group here.

A thronged room throbbing with an unimaginable din made the coffee break less than memorable. When the group reassembled a few of the writers read extracts from their work, much of which could be loosely described as memoir. All of it seemed to have been self-published. Copies of the work were displayed and, as there was no audience at the time, I hoped that they were not expecting too much of a response from me. However, I bought a novel and a CD later.

One lady, Blanche Williams, talked about her CD, which was called *How to Design Your Mind for Greatness*. She spoke of her earlier life and how she had overcome much difficulty. A presenter of a weekly radio satellite programme from New York, she asked me later to write a piece for her show, but we never got beyond the talking stage, mainly due to my lethargy.

In the afternoon all the activities were moved outdoors to a playing field, and those whom I had met earlier performed again on a stage. My interest began to wane. I phoned Dondra, who came down in a flash, surveyed the scene and introduced herself to almost everyone in sight. It was a fairly protracted leave-taking.

Later, when I was discussing the day with some Irish-American friends, there was a suggestion that I might have overstepped the racial divide. This prompted some heated if not quite acrimonious interaction but, like so much of alcohol-fuelled debate, no real satisfactory conclusion was reached. All the participants that I encountered were welcoming. Many asked me about my own writing, and some could not understand why I didn't have a business card.

It was all fairly relaxed and friendly, without a trace of hostility. I didn't feel that I had crossed any real boundaries, and often these are imagined. Maybe I wasn't the best judge on the day.

34

A BIT OF A POET

In the early 1960s a distinguished-looking gentleman knocked on the window of the Customs and Excise office in Wexford town. The window was opened by the incumbent Excise Officer, Padraic Fallon.

'Are you not coming to lunch?'

'The Collector is here.' (The Regional Manager was hidden from view in a corner of the room.)

The colourful and bawdy response from the caller on the street cannot be repeated for reasons of propriety, but Padraic's reply was less than spontaneous – he had a severe speech stammer, which added a touch of black humour to the episode: 'I can – hardly – tell – him – that', uttered as he closed the window with some deliberation.

It is not known if the pair met for a belated lunch but there is no doubt about the veracity of the incident, as it was narrated by the 'concealed' Collector himself, who was more than a little amused. The caller was the then Justice Donagh MacDonagh, poet, playwright and broadcaster son of the executed 1916 leader Thomas MacDonagh.

Padraic Fallon was born in Athenry, Co. Galway, in 1905; his father was a cattle dealer and the family owned a hotel and a butchering business. He was a boarder at Ballinasloe College and with the Cistercians in Roscrea before entering the Customs and Excise at eighteen. There is a commemorative sculpture *The Winged Horse* by his son Conor in St John's Park in Athenry. Padraic married a Cork lady, Dorothea Maher; they moved to Wexford, where they raised six sons.

Fallon spent twenty-four years as a 'Gentleman of the Excise' in Wexford; the title originated in an almost prehistoric era and was borne by other esteemed writers including Robbie Burns and Maurice Walsh. It suggested something akin to an idyllic official existence. A contemporary quoted Padraic's unsubstantiated claim that he never knew the name of the reigning Revenue Commissioner, as he never reached the end of any official instruction.

In 1963 a heavy-set, broad-shouldered man with a shock of white hair and horn-rimmed spectacles appeared in the Customs section of the Foreign Parcels Post Office in Dublin. Impeccably dressed, complete with bow tie, Padraic Fallon was a striking figure. He had transferred from Wexford.

The move to Dublin landed him in a very busy office with over a hundred officials from two departments. It was a dust-filled and parcel-clogged space with an unceasing din. It was an enormous adjustment on an official and personal level. However, a fortuitous vacancy in what was known as the Book Scale allowed him what was a sinecure of sorts, examining imported books under the Censorship of Publications Act. It was a delicious irony that one of the most distinguished poets signed the appropriate official referral to the Censorship Board. An extremely diligent and conservative post office sorter had organised the local system so that anything remotely sexual in tone would be banged off to Dublin Castle. Padraic Fallon signed on the dotted line. My belief is that he rarely read a single line from the Mickey Spillane thrillers or anything else either.

I was rarely without a book in my pocket, which often provoked a discussion. While we talked about novels and plays, we never got around to poetry as I had no idea of the extent of his achievements then. Donal O'Neill, late of Kilkenny Excise, wrote a piece in *Ireland's Own* which described his early encounters with Fallon in the 1950s – his own uneven West Cork accent and Fallon's speech impediment led to some amusing moments.

Once he was described by a senior colleague as 'a bit of poet'. It was the type of dismissive comment often thrown about thoughtlessly. Fallon was indeed a poet, one of great power and vision.

Published widely, his work appeared regularly in most of the literary journals here and in the UK including *The Dublin Magazine*, *The Bell*, *New Statesman* and *The Nation*. He was befriended by George Russell (AE), who encouraged him very much with his earlier writing and invited Padraic to his literary gatherings. According to Fallon's son, Russell became a powerful influence on the poet.

Remarkably, his collected works appeared only a few months before his death in 1974. A further edition with an introduction by Seamus Heaney and edited by the poet's son Brian, who was art critic in the *Irish Times*, appeared in 1990. It gives a great insight into the life and work of the poet.

Fallon's poetry may not be very well known today, but his reputation is secure in so far as that goes; his poetry was seen by Heaney and others as being in the same arena as that of Patrick Kavanagh and Austin Clarke. I see him in an elevated place of his own.

Acclaimed as a radio dramatist, his plays featured regularly on the BBC and Radio Éireann in the 1950s and 1960s. *Diarmuid agus Gráinne* and *The Vision of Mac Coingloinne* were rebroadcast several times and contained some of the most remarkable verse heard from either station.

A stage play, *The Seventh Step* – a tragedy in classical Greek form but set in twentieth-century Ireland – was performed in Cork and Dublin to great acclaim in 1954. A letter from Seamus Kelly ('Quidnunc', drama critic of the *Irish Times*) was found in the safe in the Excise office in Wexford thirty years later.

Letter from 'Quidnunc' to Padraic Fallon

Padraic always deflected questions about his writing. Asked about his script for a film transmitted by RTE in 1966 to commemorate the 1916 Rising and the literature of the period, he grimaced and said: 'It could have been a lot better.'

In 1967 he stepped out of a telephone kiosk in Westmoreland Street in Dublin at about 8 p.m., greeting me effusively; he was bothered that he had failed to reach his son Brian.

'They never answer the phone in that place – I'll have to go over, and I hate going in there.' It was the last time we met.

Many writers and artists visited Fallon in Wexford. Austin Clarke, Tony O'Malley, Donagh MacDonagh and Frederick May were regulars. One can imagine the spirited talk long into the night. He gave Tony O'Malley a copy of the *New Statesman* in which O'Malley learned of the artists' colony in St Ives, Cornwall, where he later spent many years.

Fallon, having retired from the Customs and Excise, moved to Cornwall – near Penzance, where his artist son Conor had settled. However, he returned in 1971 and lived happily in Kinsale. While visiting his son Ivan in Kent he became ill, and he died in Aylesford in 1974, a few months short of his seventieth birthday. His body was taken back to Kinsale, where he is buried in sight of the Atlantic.

When he died a copy of a book on studies of the religions of the ancient world was found on his desk; it lay open at a chapter on Gnosticism. On his typewriter was a translation of Rimbaud's 'Ô Saisons, ô châteaux', two lines of which are engraved on his tombstone:

> I have made a magic study
> Of the good things that elude nobody.

These lines can be taken as a summation of a poetic odyssey of half a century.

35

THE EXCISE MAN

It was six o'clock in the morning, still dark outside with some ominous grey clouds hanging heavily above the town. I was looking out from the brewhouse on the third storey of the local brewery. The early morning beer collection was slightly overdue.

I was the representative of the State with all the official paraphernalia, most of which had been inherited from Her Majesty's Government. The Excise Man had been operating in breweries for centuries. Officialdom had been very clever in inventing a legally backed system which compelled the brewer to run its operations in a manner that allowed full access to officials, even requiring a permanent office for the Excise official on site. Under these draconian regulations the brewing was monitored, measured and assessed. Finally the duty on the beer was paid over to the State on demand every month. The State took its coin painlessly.

The final process in the brewing cycle was known officially as the Declaration. The beer contained in large calibrated vats was measured with a steel dipping rod marked in tenths of an inch and with the aid of corresponding mathematical tables showing the capacity of the vats. The strength of the unfermented beer was established by representative samples drawn from the vats, which were measured with a hydrometer.

On this particular morning some calculation at an earlier stage had gone astray. I was dreaming idly as I gazed out over the surrounding rooftops, recalling some of my predecessors who had performed the same tasks down the years, some of whom I had met while based in the Guinness breweries in Dublin and Dundalk. It was a noble tradition graced by those, like Robbie Burns and Maurice Walsh, better known for their literary prowess, but also those quiet, dedicated, almost anonymous officials who had transferred from the British service.

As I waited it struck me that there was some similarity between what was happening here and the clandestine activities of the drug pushers. They gathered to carve up their products, weighing, measuring and sampling. Their working conditions would be a lot less acceptable. Later they would gather to 'split the take' with far less ceremony. The essential difference was the legitimacy of alcohol as a socially acceptable drug, formalised by my presence.

The brewery official interrupted my reverie. They were ready to proceed. The dipping and the sampling were completed. I performed the same tasks and agreement was reached. The formal declaration by the clerk was countersigned and the matter concluded. Subsequently there would be an agreed monthly figure on which the duty assessment was based. There was a further comparison of predictable yields on the brewing materials declared.

As we negotiated the rickety stairways of the brewhouse, I casually mentioned my theory of the comparison to the pushers to the Shift Manager, Jimmy Rhatigan. Looking at me slightly askance, he said

'Are you not sleeping too well these nights?'

In 1995 I produced a demand for a figure slightly in excess of £5 million in respect of the duty for one month. It was issued on a tiny official yellow form that mocked the enormity of the demand. It was never mentioned, but I always suspected that the company secretary almost shuddered at the sight of the pathetic little document, and with some justification.

The introduction of a new system of duty collection based on production and deliveries made the presence of Excise staff unnecessary – changing a centuries-old practice and relying on the ubiquitous audit under a directive from the EU.

During relief work in breweries in the late 1960s, I became forcefully aware of the extent of the dependency of the State on the Excise return from alcohol. There was a phone call from the Department of Finance looking for the production figures on the last day of the month. When I queried the necessity to have these so soon, the reply was simple: 'How do you think we will know if we can run the country?' It so happened on the first occasion that I didn't have the final calculations completed, so there was a period of uncertainty that the man had not previously experienced and he was surprised at my lack of concern.

The amounts collected in the late 1960s were considerable then, but by today's standards they appear almost infinitesimal.

In 2010 the Excise duty on beer was €836 million and that on tobacco products was €1.98 billion – staggering figures by any standard.

All of this revenue is collected with very little outlay by the State: under the system operated by Excise Officers, only three were operating in the very large breweries and when I delivered the demand for £5 million, all of the survey work and the resulting calculations were dealt with by me. At that time five qualified accountants and myriad accounts and production staff were employed at the brewery.

'You are a man alone' was the comment of one senior brewery official. There is little doubt that I felt it at times, but nonetheless I always enjoyed the work and the place.

My suggestion to the brewery official that there is a similarity between the 'drug pushers' and the brewery production of alcohol is really not that implausible. Alcohol, as stated, is a socially acceptable drug which is highly addictive, and the consequences of this addiction are a matter of daily discussion.

Strangely enough, this theory never gets much of a response when I trot it out. I wonder why?

Gentleman of the Excise

36

SHAPING

There was quite a crowd milling around the notice board in the hallway of the local Vocational School. It was September and the annual thirst for new skills had induced these eager students away from TV sets. There was a vast range of subjects available: astronomy, ballroom dancing Latin American style, guitar lessons, creative writing and interior design, apart from the more practical subjects like accountancy and modern languages.

Lured by the mysticism of the East, I was interested in enrolling for yoga. Room 17, the board said, but to my surprise a lengthy queue had already formed. Shortly afterwards the teacher appeared and announced that only the first twelve would be enrolled. It was simply a matter of space.

My second choice was pottery, and this class turned out to be a relaxed, informal group of about twelve, mainly comprising young women. We were introduced to the workings of the clay and, with the minimum of instruction, largely left to our own devices. I was aware of a great air of activity around me. Everyone seemed to have a clear idea of what they wished to form. Soap dishes, vases and ashtrays and many other functional items slowly began to emerge over the first few weeks. Once they came out of the kiln fully formed, there was much satisfaction all round. Eventually I managed a crudely shaped soap dish, but mostly I was content to mould and remould large lumps of clay into circular, ill-defined shapes. They resembled human heads without any of the normal accoutrements.

I was content to sit there; the slow, repetitive movements of my hands were relaxing and calming. No one took any notice, apart from an occasional encouraging smile from the teacher.

I looked forward to the two-hour class each week. The industry of the group left me unmoved. While I was impressed by their skill, I continued to sit quietly moulding and kneading. Shapes like ears, eyes and noses appeared and disappeared. Then one week a shape – a recognisable head – emerged. It was not quite normal, maybe a bit distorted, but yet a human head. It was still incomplete; it did not have a mouth.

It was turned in for setting and fired in the kiln. The following week when it reappeared it looked even stranger. The rest of the class was in raptures admiring their various items. Undeniably they were good – some astonishingly so. My head was unremarked upon.

Over the next few weeks I produced some more heads. They were fashioned slowly and carefully and almost lovingly. One common factor was the singular lack of a mouth. The teacher asked about this in a very gentle, indirect way, but I was unable to offer anything of any consequence. It seemed nothing more needed to be said.

Eventually I moved on a little, and very slowly and almost painfully I produced two figures gazing at each other on what could loosely be described as a log. Only one of the figures had a mouth. A few hours in the kiln solidified them.

They now sit gazing at each other on a small table in my sittingroom, accompanied by four strange human heads. All are silent, sitting happily. They are rarely remarked upon. It seems to me that they have encouraged quietness in the room. They provoke strange ideas in my head at times, but I keep the thoughts to myself, remaining silent. Most of the time.

37

RUNNING FOR GLORY OR SURVIVAL?

The doctor turned back at the bedroom door.

'Are you still at the jogging?'

'Yeah, but I call myself a runner.'

Instantly I knew it sounded daft.

'Great stuff – well, I don't jog or even walk if I can avoid it, I smoke and drink but I'd say that I'm in far better shape than you are now.' His laughter rounded it off as he left.

I felt a right clown, on top of the bronchitis that he had diagnosed. I had walked into the trap that assailed so many middle-aged joggers. When eventually I told the Belfield group – Maurice Twomey, Brendan Murphy and a few others – there was no more than tolerant smiles as a response. That day I noticed there was very little talk on the run; in fact I felt the strain and struggled to keep up with the pace. The silence was the real giveaway – talking and hard breathing don't go too well together at a sharp pace. It was of course the perfect response to my aspirations.

Hours and hours had been spent in the grounds of the university – one could use the track also. The training for the first two Dublin Marathons in 1980 and 1981 was negotiated on those laborious laps, as well as the New York Marathon in 1983. Running down 5th Avenue at the twenty-mile stage I was astounded to see Maree screaming her support. It was a great moment, which I celebrated by hugging her: she was with some of the other partners who had been undecided whether to watch the race on TV because of the torrential rain.

New York Marathon, 1983

The 'highs' and the release of the famous endorphins were all necessary, as the constant auld slog was unbelievably tedious at times. Training prior to the marathon, a twenty-mile run was recommended a month or so prior to the event. In Marlay Park, up the road from where we then lived, on a Sunday about 10.30 a.m. a schoolboys' soccer game was starting. As I trundled on the circuit they duly finished and were replaced by another two teams. This second group had finished before I completed my twenty miles. That day it got to me, struggling on my own as Maurice, my usual partner on long runs, was unavailable – round and round as so many people came and left the park. Was it worth all this straining? The answer was elusive, but it was probably a good example of the loneliness of the long-distance runner.

On a memorable occasion but a more joyful morning, Kevin, David and the Queen, alias Niamh, were on the track and attempting to lure me into a race when my father came down and silently ran along with the rest of us. Three generations together for a few yards, but we all knew that this was hugely significant and my Dad, with his creaking hip, in his mid-seventies, was simply very happy. No need for endorphins there.

The only person missing from that group was of course Maree. Without her unfailingly great support it could not have taken place. It was not easy for her, yet she never complained. One Saturday in mid-winter during the cross-country season a lady phoned and asked Maree if she knew what time we could be expected back from Bray. Her sister and the brother-in-law were running with me.

'I'm not sure really; not for a while yet, but one never knows – on a race day it could run into tomorrow.'

This offering was met with a deafening silence.

Meanwhile we were skulling celebratory pints in Byrne's of Galloping Green.

There was very little literature available on running when the 'running boom' began in the late 1970s. In midsummer of 1980, RTE Radio 2 began broadcasting a ten-minute slot on a Monday evening. Jimmy Greeley's input was eagerly awaited by runners who were largely inexperienced, particularly over long distances.

In August 1982 there was a shy, very tentative approach by a man in the dressing room prior to the fifteen-mile race around the lakes in Mullingar. The scene was a little unusual – mainly middle-aged men rubbing various solutions on parts of their bodies not normally adorned. Vaseline mainly, but some were not averse to oils being liberally applied to every part that moved.

'What are they all rubbing on and … [he barely got it out] … Why?'

He stared in disbelief when I explained the results of friction on the tender parts of the body and the constant movement of gear over two or three hours … I am sure that I was the first person to advise him that he should be particularly careful of his nipples: 'Lash it on.' He recoiled, plainly embarrassed, when I offered the Vaseline jar. 'Everything that moves' was my last piece of advice.

Many people were swept up by the romantic running hysteria and were simply unprepared for the consequences. It didn't take too long for me to recognise that to forget the toes was a serious omission, which conveys nothing of the resulting havoc. The need for a regular intake of water was learned pretty quickly by many, but still it took some quite a while to cop on.

The danger of dehydration was a constant, and even experienced runners were taken unawares at times.

Gradually the influence of Jim Fixx and his *Complete Book of Running* spread across the Atlantic. The American journalist who discovered running while an overweight forty-year-old lured thousands of Americans back into physical activity. The American cardiologist George Sheehan, who gave up his practice at forty-five to concentrate on running, also inspired many with his philosophical thoughts mixed with running advice in five books. *Running and Being* is a magical volume which really pushed me into a totally different way of appreciating exercise. Sheehan toured the western hemisphere, running in races and lecturing. He came to Dublin in 1983 and I watched him running in the rain with Noel Carroll in Belfield one Saturday morning.

One Saturday afternoon, on my way home from some kind of work or other, I togged off in Belfield and headed out the side gate up the hill towards Mount Merrion. Two ladies apparently in distress with their car asked for my help. I handed my car keys to one of them to hold. The problem was solved in a few minutes; I parked the car and headed off on my run. Suddenly I stopped: I had no keys, and heading back down the hill I was feeling very nervous. What would they do with my keys? It was an official car – I began to wonder what in God's name I would tell them in the office. 'Gave the car to an American lady.'

'We didn't know what to do,' and they laughed. Too close for comfort.

'Running keeps me sane' was my constant refrain. I believed it did, particularly as I was in the wrong job, even though I made the best of it. Running, squash and pipe smoking, together with the most wonderfully placid lady, Maree, made the difference. Not a bad combination.

38

A PHONE CALL

It was about ten o'clock on a cold February morning. I had just finished a leisurely breakfast when the silence was broken by the shrill-sounding phone. A female voice said quietly: 'Are you Frank Marshall, and do you have a daughter called Niamh?'

There was something strange about the slow, deliberate nature of the questions. I was instantly uneasy. My mind began to race ahead, and I felt distinctly edgy.

The caller said she was ringing from the Court House in Kilkenny. This information added to my unease. Only a few brief moments had elapsed. The caller had uttered three sentences and I was almost immobilised with fear. My imagination was in overdrive.

The caller announced that Niamh, who was based in Brussels, was entitled to a Diplomatic vote, adding that the voting card had been posted in error to my address instead of being sent by courier to the Department of Foreign Affairs. It was clear that there was a minor panic about complicated official procedure, and she wished to collect the voting card. As a former official I was sympathetic, and we came to an agreeable arrangement.

Relaxed at this stage, I told the lady that Niamh was somewhere in the foothills of Ben Nevis with two companions and was almost certainly totally unconcerned about voting procedures. Later when she called to collect the card I mentioned the shock I had got when the questions were posed in such an officious tone. She understood, and admitted that she could have handled it differently.

It had all worked out fine in the end, but on reflection, while I knew that I had over-reacted, there was the undeniable fact that some people get phone calls with shattering news that dramatically changes their lives. I was lucky.

Niamh was amused when I related the story. That morning they were struggling in driving snow near the summit of Ben Nevis. The weather softened and the crisis passed. They made it to the summit. They continued climbing in the vicinity all week.

There was a time when it seemed Niamh was spending more time on the mountains than elsewhere. An extended session in the Atlas Mountains in Morocco was strenuous, but the deprivation of the normal comforts was the real problem. Hiring a guide in Slovenia led to her conquering the highest peak there, Mount Triglav. She climbed in Austria and Switzerland, and of course the home peaks were not neglected.

One evening in a gym in Brussels I was astonished at her preparation on one of those indoor climbing walls. When I remarked on this later she admonished me about my focusing on heights; we had read and discussed *The Beckoning Silence* by Joe Simpson, the English climber, and it had made me very conscious of the real dangers of climbing.

'You're too hung up on heights, Dad' – and really that was the problem. It passed, as did Niamh's interest in climbing.

She did not escape the 'hurling fever' which is beyond immunisation in some families. It was inevitable that she would succumb to the Kilkenny drug, particularly as she knew the history of her paternal grandfather's addiction to the Black and Amber. Yet I was astonished when one Sunday after last mass I saw the Kikenny flag floating freely from the top window of our house. All I could do was laugh – it had been there since the previous evening when she left to go to the All-Ireland Final

'It's in my genes, Dad.'

In the end I gave in gracefully, more or less.

August Weekend
(for Niamh)

Thinking of you heading towards Clifden
reminder of a weekend in 1962 in Clare.
One year younger than you.
Can you imagine me at twenty-three?

The weekend Marilyn Monroe died
Alone. 'If I must be on my own
I want to be by myself' she said in one
of her less than memorable films.

Still mourned, provoking much debate
among the now middle-aged; her memory
kept alive by profiteers and scandalmongers.
Lonely was her middle name.

She brought many men to the edge
yet couldn't turn back herself; maybe
all too distant as you skirt around
the West on a sombre August anniversary

39

BEHIND THE BLUE DOOR

I didn't really know where I was when the phone woke me: its shrill insistence sounded more like an alarm. I croaked a word into the receiver.

'Hello Frank, is that you? This is Robin from the office.'

'Who?'

'Robin. Sorry to wake you but the Boss said to ring you, the office is on fire.'

'What?!' I screamed.

'Yeah, a shagging blaze, Fire Brigade, the whole shebang.'

'Why are you ringing me?'

'You're a key holder.'

This made no sense whatsoever, as it was the first time that I was told of my exalted status of key holder. Many years later Robin told me that he was instructed to tell everyone on the night that they were key holders.

'Anyway, Frank, the Boss wants you to go in immediately – just gone 4 a.m. now.'

It was hard to grasp, and a creeping unease didn't help. My running gear was in the office. I had been running to and from home and office. Like many runners, my sense of value was really focused: the possibility of losing a new pair of running shoes was uppermost in my mind. The absurdity gripped me as I stumbled out of the sack and headed for the bathroom.

About 40 minutes later I was stopped by a uniformed Garda.

'You can't go down there, Sir.'

'I work in the building.'

His response was lost as I caught my first glimpse of what was once a majestic three-storey Georgian structure over a basement, with eight steps to a dark blue door. The most striking sight was the huge mound of smoking debris heaped in the front garden, about six feet high and growing as a stream of stuff poured down from the gaping black holes which were all that remained of the windows. The cumulative effect of smoke and water had drastically defaced the front of the building. In the back garden there was less activity, but the pervasive acrid smell of burning seemed strangely stronger.

Two of my colleagues stood silently, clearly shocked, reflecting my own state. We really didn't have much to say.

A uniformed Garda came over and produced a brown leather wallet.

'Would any of you know who the owner might be?'

I recognised it instantly as belonging to a colleague with whom I worked and travelled regularly. It was always bulging – the subject of much mirth.

'How are you so sure?' Paddy asked.

'Sure I'm tired of looking at it – the fattest one in the house.'

When I told the Guard, he asked that I would ensure its safe return.

We were allowed back into the building later in the morning. There was an indescribable shambles in the basement and ground floor, with water and debris swirling everywhere, all overlaid with a disgusting aroma of stale smoke. Floor boards were lifted on the first floor, outside my office, but I managed to get into the room. It was untouched except for scorched floor coverings and smashed windows; my flashy tracksuit lay on a filing cabinet and the running shoes beamed up at me from the corner.

The back of the house was largely undamaged but the front rooms were beyond redemption. Peering cautiously into the front room off our landing, I was amazed to see Barney labouring feverishly, throwing boxes and files into the enormous heap in the front garden.

'What are you at?'

'What the hell do you think? This is the best chance to get rid of all the tricky overdue files. A gift from the Gods, up to date in one strike – shag them all out – now or never.'

He was almost enjoying himself: I couldn't believe what I was seeing. 'Lost in fire' was the refrain endlessly quoted on many reports from that day on.

The wallet was duly handed back to its rightful owner, but not before the contents were revealed as, *inter alia*, three uncashed salary cheques, US dollars and no shortage of punts. It became a kind of stale joke – eventually all the amounts were exaggerated ridiculously. The owner was pleased to get it back, and left a box of tennis balls on my desk much later.

I was sad to see a beautiful house destroyed, though luckily there was no loss of life. It was later established that it was arson, but of course never fully proved. It was the house of two tea clubs, three grades and constant bickering and spitefulness, and most of all childish inter-grade pettiness. Yet it had some gloriously happy memories. Many very successful investigations were completed there by men of outstanding brilliance and commitment. In all my time in the various locations it was pretty standard to find highly competent officials. However, the men in the top floor tea club were exceptionally bright and committed.

One official with a great sense of the ridiculous coined the immortal phrase 'No goodbye kisses and no hot dinners' when urgently summoning his staff to leave the office at very short notice. Once the Shannon was crossed the urgency often evaporated miraculously, and steaks and pints were set upon; of course much work was eventually done.

We never got back in to the house with the lovely blue door. I moved on to pastures new in Kilkenny within the year. There is much sadness in reflecting on the many really fine men there who died prematurely. I never missed the place as I was never really right for it, but I survived and actually enjoyed some of the many investigation trips that took me to the UK: Manchester and the midlands around Birmingham and Northampton were traversed endlessly on these trips. It was often hard, demanding work accompanied by the British investigation officers, who were extremely diligent. It was amazing just how many people claimed that they were unaware that the completion of export declarations involved certain consequences about the availability of their records.

On one UK ten-day trip, one of the local officials drove me endlessly around the North East in his own car, for which he was paid a mileage allowance. I was invited to his home before I left; his wife said 'You will never know what you have done for us – this travel allowance is just a life saver now.'

All I could do was smile, being slightly embarrassed by her genuine gratitude. Her husband, who was a great guy, laughingly said: 'Don't put it in the official report, Frank.'

The official visits to Northern Ireland were not exactly pleasure cruises, and it was hard to see the unending struggle and constant pressure the ordinary people were subjected to in the midst of the Troubles. It was sobering on a Monday morning in Derry city when an accountant turned to me and said: 'Can I see your ID again?' Handing it back, he tried to smile. 'We don't often get men with black leather coats and short haircuts in here.' The message was not lost on me.

My life was threatened in the course of my work and the culprit taken to court, but the matter was bungled in court and unresolved.

It was easy to move on when the time came. Kilkenny seemed like the Promised Land by comparison.

40

WHO DID WRITE *ULYSSES*?

I was searching for something or other on my bookshelves, and came across a very old copy of *Dubliner* magazine dated July/August 1962. The contents were listed as Reviews, Arts, Plays and Controversies. I noticed the name Niall Montgomery and familiar bells began to ring. On page 11, I read 'Proust and Joyce: a lecture by Niall Montgomery'; a footnote said this was a transcription from a tape recording of a lecture given in the Building Centre, Dublin, on Friday 22 June 1962, during Joyce Week.

I remembered sitting at the back of the hall in the basement of the Building Centre on the night in question. I didn't recall too much about the lecture, but Niall Montgomery was a tall, thin, ascetic-looking man with a fine clear voice, indeed a commanding presence. The late Donagh MacDonagh was chairman, and there was a third man on the platform whose identity I cannot recall. It was a disturbance that occurred towards the end of the evening that was responsible for my vivid recollection of events.

The lecture was finished, and Donagh MacDonagh was taking questions from the audience of about a hundred people. A low-sized bald man carrying a raincoat appeared at the back of the hall. I was not aware of his presence during the lecture, and I had the impression that he had arrived late. Suddenly, in a loud, raucous voice he said: 'I don't know what the effin' hell ye are all going on about; it's a well-known fact that I wrote the bloody book *Ulysses* and indeed I'm the only one capable of writing it.'

There was a sudden electrifying silence. Everyone turned around to see who had made this startling interjection. My companion nudged me and whispered: 'You know who your man is?'

When I stared at him blankly he continued: 'Myles na gCopaleen – Flann O'Brien.'

At this stage there was a huge stir in the hall: some people had clearly recognised him and were waiting expectantly for a response from the panel. It was not to come. The Chairman consulted with Niall Montgomery, stood up thanked him for an excellent contribution and the audience for their attention, and concluded the proceedings with more than some haste. It seemed likely that Myles was fortified to some extent at the time ...

It was a dramatic and unexpected ending. I was disappointed that there was no response to Myles's claim that he was the author of *Ulysses*. My companion and I were expecting some hilarious response in what could have been a lively debate. However, it was clear that the panel believed that it would have been unwise to take on Myles on this topic. He was being deliberately provocative and he would have been irrepressible with his caustic wit, mercilessly slaying the opposition. Maybe they were right to finish the proceedings quickly. The crowd dispersed slowly: I can't remember if Myles left immediately. I thought about his comic masterpiece *At Swim-Two-Birds*, and could imagine his claim settling easily into that outrageously funny book.

I told the story of the incident to a man I encountered in the Cistercian Abbey in Mount Melleray in the late 1960s. Apparently both of them drank occasionally in the White Horse bar on Burgh Quay. He had great time for Myles, or Brian O'Nolan – his real name. Myles was stimulating company, but like many a man often became a bit obstreperous with more than a sup on board.

My friend took Myles back to his house for a nightcap. He left in good shape but without his famous raincoat. He knew nothing about this omission until Myles called to retrieve the coat, of which there was no trace. The lady of the house had dumped it without a word to her husband. She told Myles with great conviction that it must have been left elsewhere.

Myles was less than happy, but a few balls of malt settled him on the night. My friend was embarrassed, but more significantly he feared Myles might write up the incident in his Cruiskeen Lawn column in the *Irish Times*. He was sure he would not be named, but felt that the scribe was so masterful that he could subtly reveal a clue to the couple's identity. It didn't happen, and they lived happily – for a while anyway. None of the principals would now be alive, and one wonders how many of the modern generation are familiar with the writer and his celebrated satirical tomes.

41

THE LAST TRIP

It was 2008; David had successfully got a position as an Addiction Therapist and was ready to return to Dublin after eighteen years in the USA. It was an occasion of some celebration. Having made seventeen trips across the Atlantic, I wanted simply to go once more – just like all big children. As it turned out it was difficult enough to arrange, but in April I flew out to Louisville in Kentucky *en route* to the Cistercian Monastery of Our Lady of Gethsemani, where Fr Louis, better known as Thomas Merton, had spent his monastic life.

I was there to join a retreat based on the poetry of Mary Oliver and Thomas Merton in the Thomas Merton Institute, about a mile from the monastery. I joined four ladies from Louisville – Episcopalians – and an Irish-American lady. The facilitator was Jonathan Montaldo, a writer and editor, and a prominent layman in the Thomas Merton Society. There was some focus on the relative poetic merits of the two writers and we were showered with handouts, but to be very honest the literary aspect was lightly skated over. The exploration of Faith and the thirst for real experience of a Personal God dominated the proceedings. This was a genuine deep-rooted desire which had been pursued by these ladies over a number of years. In fairness to the facilitator, he allowed this searching exploration to develop.

The highlight of the retreat was a visit to Merton's Hermitage in the Monastic Enclosure. At 5.30 on a cold grey morning we moved gingerly in the half light on a circuitous route over a dirt track which eventually opened into a long, narrow field surrounded with majestic redwoods. The Hermitage, a wooden one-storey structure with a veranda, looked oddly out of place, as if someone had just dropped it in the middle of a large farm. We knew it was a rare privilege to be there and we were aware of the central part it had played in the monk's life, about which so much had been written.

Retreatants including the author at Merton's Hermitage, Kentucky, 2008

Thomas Merton withdrew from the community in the abbey and lived a life of seclusion there. The supreme irony was the growth of his fame that coincided with his withdrawal. This move was not entirely supported by the Abbot, with whom there was a less than even relationship.

The seven of us sat in silence on the veranda and just gazed down through the slowly emerging light. We became aware of barely perceptible movements at the top of the field. A few deer were prancing around in the half light. Jonathan was a man of action and never missed an opportunity, so I was asked to read from Merton's beautiful poem 'Hagia Sophia'.

> ... There is in all things an inexhaustible sweetness and purity, a silence that is a fount of action and joy. It rises up in wordless gentleness ... I am awakened, I am born again at the voice of this, my Sister, sent to me from the depths of the divine fecundity ...

Highly emotive language, and then we sat there with our thoughts; mine floated restlessly around the tragic accident that caused the monk's sudden death during a break in a conference in Bangkok, where he was pursuing his interest in Buddhism. There was something very poignant in the fact that he died because of a malfunctioning electrical device having travelled across the globe – after years of silent meditation in Kentucky.

Having spent some time in the living quarters – one room and a bathroom, each sparsely but adequately furnished – we left and strolled back to the monastery now visible across the fields. It was easy to imagine Fr Louis treading the same path over the years. We visited his grave before leaving the Enclosure. It was marked by a cross which bore his name – Father Louis Merton – and the date of his death, 10 December 1968 (he was 53).

Once the others had departed I spent another four days in a hermitage in the garden behind the Retreat Centre. A veranda overlooked a lake which was visited by innumerable rare birds. A book featuring the birds of the area and binoculars helped to identify the mellifluous sounds ringing out all day. Early morning meditation was just a little different form the surroundings at home.

A thunder and lightning storm with an indescribable crashing din and terrifying flashing light invaded the hermitage at about 4 o'clock one morning. It was a bewildering shock. Probably for the first time I discovered how powerless we are in the face of the elements. It disappeared almost as quickly as it came, leaving an eerie silence.

I moved on that day, and was happy to be in the relative peace of Palm Beach, which had been the recent centre of hurricane territory but fortunately not just then. Early morning swims off the beach were always on my own, as the locals used their own pools. To one who was a regular on the Bull Wall in Dollymount and the Forty Foot in Sandycove, 'those artificial yokes' held no attraction!

I had two nights in Florida, which I knew well enough not to want to hang around for longer, even though David had an apartment on Ocean Boulevard. I headed for Washington, DC. Having been there only once previously, I had not seen the Vietnam Veterans Memorial. I had been of an age with many of the young conscripts who were sent to the fiercely bitter cauldron of Vietnam in the 1960s. It was hard to ignore the suffering and slaughter as portrayed on the TV then.

My visit to Washington coincided with the visit of Pope John Paul to the city, which made moving around quite difficult, particularly in the vicinity of the National Mall where the memorial wall is situated. The Veterans Memorial pays tribute to those who were killed or listed as missing in action during the conflict. A total of 58,209 servicemen are listed in chronological order of the date of the casualty. The names are etched in black letters on the wall, which is 10 metres at its highest, tapering to height 20 cm.

Mere statistics can never catch the meaning or symbolism of the events commemorated. Just walking by, observing small groups of people gathering at a spot with heads bowed, says all that is needed. I found it very moving, and I knew not a soul listed yet I could not escape the sadness and the bleakness. An overwhelming sense of pointless loss hung about, and yet one cannot take from the valour and real commitment involved. Yet the unanswerable question remained – what difference did it all make?

As I moved away I saw the large bronze statues depicting three young servicemen and a separate large sculpture of two women in uniform tending to the wounds of a male soldier, both of which were constructed around the same time as the wall to honour the many men and women who served in the conflict.

There is a war memorial in Hanoi commemorating those who served on the Vietnamese side. The number of casualties is unknown.

After a brief stay in Washington I returned to see David safely off the shores on which he had famously come into his own. I flew out four hours later, having failed to get on the same flight. My peregrinations over the two weeks had involved ten flights in all, as flying Continental Airlines on the east coast involves each one calling to the headquarters in Atlanta. I had a few close encounters as I hared up and down the airport corridors making deadlines.

42

NO MORE PIPE, GRANDAD, FIRE ALL GONE

It was a very good feeling to see my name in the contents page of the Dominican publication *Spirituality* for the fourth time. Casually glancing at the other contributions, my gaze stopped suddenly at 'Spirituality and Health – Smoking' by Joe Armstrong. It was a very significant moment, and deep within me there was a disturbing unease.

Later I read it, and was appalled at its tone: there was a challenging directness that irritated me; a clear reasoned logic which argued that a believing Christian was on the wrong track inhaling poisonous smoke that would eventually ruin one's health. I read it again and still felt it was rubbish. Deep down I knew it was almost undeniable, but pipe smokers didn't inhale ... I knew I was clutching at straws after forty-five years of pipe smoking since January 1958. I had felt for some time that it was not doing me any good and was probably causing a lot of harm.

The article offered an invitation to work online free of charge with anyone interested in quitting. I thought about it a lot, discussed it with Maree, prayed about it and cursed the whole idea, but finally sent what I thought was an amusing email to Joe Armstrong. He responded positively and explained the programme. He would work with me over six months. After a short period of reflection I took it on. When I expressed some doubt about the withdrawal symptoms, Joe asked 'Are you not a man of faith?'

The good news was that I would not have to quit until the first day of the fifth week. A whole month of smoking – sure where was the problem? I smoked my head off day and night for the whole month, just like a big child.

Then on 27th October 2003 I threw three pipes into the river Nore from Ossory Bridge. That was it. On a previous attempt I had buried my pipes in the back garden but weeks later, late at night, had dug them up and began puffing again. When I related that story, a friend had remarked, 'I suppose you will be buying snorkelling equipment now.'

Dumping of pipes, Ossory Bridge, 2003

Ten years have passed, and I am still free of the pipe. I don't miss it and know that I am better off without it. The core of the programme was a commitment to early morning journaling of three A4 pages coupled with a healthy lifestyle of early rising and retiring. The support of Joe Armstrong was crucial, with endless hours of talking and talking on the phone. I learned something about the nature of addiction, eventually accepting that I was never meant to stick a hot wooden pipe full of burning tobacco in my gob six times a day and keep it there for about forty minutes each time.

I hung in with the unquenchable support of a few friends – Stephen Kelly, Colm O Doherty and the late Rev. Cecil Weeks, who held my hand in broad daylight in Kilkenny and talked about the healing power of God. Their regular emails and those from Doug Conlon in Australia helped enormously. I relied regularly on my son David in the USA; his insights were immeasurably supportive but 'Dad, your mind is playing tricks on your body and you just want to go back into the comfort zone' didn't sit too easily with me. Irascibility was a constant companion, as Maree discovered as she supported me quietly in the background.

The day before I quit I met Donagh O'Shea, a Dominican priest, at the Integritas Christian Centre outside Kilkenny. I told him my sad, weary tale and outlined the programme. I was clearly looking for a way out. He listened and said simply but benignly: 'You have made your decision then.'

His response saved me, though I was less than happy on my way home.

I got my 'fifteen minutes of fame' telling my story in a Dublin hotel when Micheál Martin, Minister for Health and Children, launched Joe Armstrong's book *Write Way to Stop Smoking*. There was a distinguished panel and a battery of TV cameramen and reporters milling around the platform, waiting not for my revelations but for the amended date of impending legislation banning smoking in hotels, restaurants and public offices. It was a novel experience, which I enjoyed, and I managed to quote my grandson Liam's comment when I showed him a photograph of him sitting on my knee as I puffed contentedly: 'No more pipe Grandad, fire all gone.'

It took about six months before the cloud of unease began to move; it was an immense, almost unutterable release to be free of talking and thinking of addiction and everything associated with it. Often I was painfully aware that I was making too much of the whole shebang, particularly with so much undisclosed suffering in the lives of many people.

Months later, at a tea break during a conference for Samaritan volunteers, I was talking to a lady from Northern Ireland and the smoking ban came up – it didn't apply there. Of course in the middle I mentioned my own recent travails. She listened intently, then looked at me and with unmistakable emotion in her voice, said: 'At least you had a choice – my husband never got one; he got cancer and died.'

Clearly very upset, she walked away. I was a bit shocked, but I actually understood. It put everything in context, but it was too late to recall all the whingeing.

Grandad's Cap in the Air

(for Heather, Liam and Jenny)

Trudging through the neatly manicured estate
in the steady drizzle of grey November.
My expectant glance rewarded by
three small eager smiling faces,
glued to upstairs window waving frantically,
dispelling any gloom instantly. Uncharacteristically
exclaiming wildly I throw my cap high in the air.
Anticipating joyous weekend of glorious company.

43

FREEDOM

It was a very bright, fresh morning in Boston. The temperature was considerably lower than Palm Beach, where we had spent the previous week with our son David. Weather was the last thing on my mind as we walked in the lobby of a building occupied by 'Eye Men'. It was a 'swish joint', suggesting very fancy fees. However, Bill O'Neill's comment, 'Haven't you a son over there and they are supposed to be the best in the world?' was uppermost in my mind.

Quietly apprehensive, I was glad Maree was with me and as we waited for the lift it struck me that this was the first time she had accompanied me in any kind of medical consultation. The clinically cold diagnosis of retinal dystrophy by a Dublin specialist had left me floundering. 'I can't do any laser work on that condition. It is incurable and there is no treatment apart from monitoring it.'

After the usual preliminary tests reading charts, we were greeted by the consultant, a courteous Bostonian, as was apparent from his soft tones. He spent a while explaining the procedures and asking very detailed questions about my lifestyle, then left us in the hands of his lady assistant. .

It was a long, wearying morning, being photographed and tested in dark rooms, but it was all done with grace and consideration. At the end the consultant asked me if I wanted the good news or the bad news first. I smiled and waited.

'Well, Sir, the heart attack will probably get you first, but you seem to be in such good condition with all the jogging and tennis, that will be a very long way down the road.'

I felt it was a prettty facile answer: we talked a bit more but it was quite clear that there were no satisfactory answers. This condition was recessive: it would need monitoring, but there might be no great change for years. Before we left he told me that as he was not a retinal specialist he had arranged an appointment for me with one in the same building on the following day.

I was not mad about the idea but agreed, and the next day began with the usual reading tests and my humour decidedly uneven. Maree told me later that this was evident and she decided not to introduce a note of levity by asking 'Who has the eye problem here?' while watching me flashing effortlessly down the chart to the last line when she could barely see the chart. The consultant smiled said not a word initially; he just began looking at the documents in his hand and eventually said: 'I see you have come from Ireland with great back–up. I see many people from your country with retinal dystrophy and I am aware that there is a lot of intermarrying in families over there.'

I couldn't believe what I was hearing. He drooled on in the same vein, and then almost instinctively I intervened: 'Excuse me, I have no doubt about your experience but I did not come over here to get a lecture in sociology, I have traced my ancestors back for nearly two hundred years and there is no trace of intermarrying.'

My words seemed to hang in the air. He made no response. Maree said later that he looked shocked, but he said: 'I think the fluorescent test would be a good idea – an X-ray followed by an injection of a coloured dye and a further X-ray.

This procedure took a while. The consultant proceeded to ask if I could come back in six months, when the test would be repeated and any change monitored. He asked an assistant to arrange a series of photographs: there was a very awkward pause before the consultant was reminded that the previous test would preclude the possibility of a true image.

Turning to me, he suggested that I make an appointment for whenever I was visiting my son 'so that we could monitor any appreciable changes in the condition'. I thanked him, and as we turned to leave he asked us to wait for a moment. He picked up the phone and began speaking in a very low voice: 'Please have a word with my secretary on your way out, and have a safe trip home.'

The secretary seemed a bit flustered as she said something about not paying the full fee as the photographs were not taken. I asked about the normal fee; her response was hesitant and nervous ...

'About $500, depending on the tests involved: if you would like to make an offer it would be acceptable.' She was clearly uneasy at this kind of wheeling and dealing. I was tempted momentarily to say 'We'll call it quits' and leave, but I mentioned a figure of $100 and her beaming smile said it all.

The visit to the USA left me vaguely unsettled, with no clearer view than an uncertain future. It didn't take long to realise that this was my ticket to freedom. I went back to the Dublin consultant, who had two reports from Boston. They were glossed over, and I said that I was thinking of retiring in six months' time. I don't think I will ever forget the moment when he said: 'You might not have six months left.'

When I asked what he meant he just shrugged his shoulders, almost impatiently.

'Well, if that condition spreads just a little it could obscure the macula and you would be left with only peripheral vision at best.'

I remained very calm with some difficulty, as I thought it a heartless, indifferent response but in character with his previous form.

'Will you certify the official form?'

He nodded as he said 'Yes'. He didn't examine me: that was it, except for the usual fee.

It took two long agonising months and two reminders before the letter arrived. I had all the necessary arrangements in place with Personnel Branch and they were sympathetic. On 18 April 1996 I drove over Ossory Bridge knowing that this was the last day of my official life.

It was strange but exhilarating, a mixture of many emotions: almost indescribable, but it was all good.

My colleagues were astonished when I told them, as only one of them knew of the eye condition. They held a retirement function when it all became official, and I was humbled by the large gathering on the night. I had mentioned the phrase 'about six months left' to one person and it went out that 'Marshall was going blind'. I was unconcerned: nothing at all could bother me then. It probably sounds a bit daft, but it felt like I had been reborn.

I was given a twelve-gear bicycle by my colleagues. I alluded to the delicious irony in that gift for a man retiring on health grounds. Eighteen years later I am still cycling on that same bike, with over ten thousand miles registered on the milometer. I have no doubt that some people think I pulled a stroke as they did not expect to see me still pedalling around. No one ever said a word except the head of the department, half jokingly but wholly in earnest.

The author, Mick Lynch and Jimmy O'Halloran: day of the GROW cycle, Kilkenny to Tipperary town, 1997

A few months later I sat down in the garden and, over a month, wrote a radio play which related the story of the disintegration of a marriage due to the strain caused by the sudden onset of the husband's blindness. The outcome is well documented herein.

There is no doubt that its emergence helped me to put aside any unconscious fears of what might lie ahead. It was a blessing in disguise, even though the play was not generally well received. The other, not unconnected, blessing is the great good fortune of eighteen years of sight, courtesy of the Good Lord. Maybe the Boston consultant was near enough in his forecast – who knows?

44

IS THAT ALL THERE IS?

The answer is resoundingly affirmative. While this is not my first attempt at this last chapter, a form of lingering unease was preventing me from letting the whole process go. Its completion is an achievement irrespective of the outcome, and that thought alone has freed me.

The unease was not unconnected to the omission of the story of my visit to Wellpinit, where my friend Jack O'Leary, an American Jesuit, was ministering to the Native American Indians on the reservation east of Spokane. Our friendship goes back to 1977 and we have met in various locations on both sides of the Atlantic. In 2006 it was a memorable experience to be part of the community despite the incessant snow fall. Jack, who had spent over forty years on the African missions, was undeterred by mere snow. It was a privilege to accompany him to the funeral on the reservation of an elderly lady who just happened to bear the same maiden name – Kenny – as Maree's late mother. 'The Irish just about reached everywhere in the USA' was Jack's wry comment.

Over the years I was blessed to be exposed to very many generous souls, both male and female, who steered me into safe havens. They helped me to an understanding of Christianity which moved me away from the behavioural model in which it seemed one had to earn everything, including the love of God. It was a slow learning process, but it was helped enormously by the person who introduced me to another influential Jesuit, Anthony de Mello. He offered a form of prayer and meditation which incorporated the riches of eastern wisdom and traditional Christian practice; over the years this led me on to the further study and practice of Tai Chi and yoga in various locations.

It wasn't all one-way traffic, as over a cumulative period of twenty-six years I was a member of various voluntary groups like the Society of St Vincent de Paul and the Samaritans, and innumerable liturgy groups. The example of my parents would have been a huge factor.

Six years in the meditation group based in Butler House in Kilkenny, where I was introduced to Tai Chi and the discipline of the Buddhist meditation, was hugely significant. I have been sustained by the support of many groups where the presence of strong, supportive women was the one constant, unchanging feature. Except in the USA, men just didn't feature. Ironically, my presence in these groups was often interpreted perversely as 'painting outside the lines'.

It was not all as serious as it might sound: there was much relaxation and fun, as generally women are light years ahead of the males in this arena.

Fortunately the other real, tangible blessing is the unfailing positivism of Maree. She has been a real antidote to my seriousness with her gentle, mocking humour, which is hard to resist. She has taught me how to laugh at myself, but ultimately she has shown me that the essence of Christianity is a love that forgives without conditions. All of this is done without a word of admonition except to emphasise the need to stay in the present moment, abandoning the enslaving past.

However, we know that this life is a transient one that will disappear, as will all that is precious in our lives, not to mention the ephemeral. The Christian message offers the unconditional love of God with the promise of Eternal life. I realise that my total acceptance of that message can be viewed as irrational and impossible to prove, but I don't have to prove it or indeed do anything else except to try and live it as best I can, with undying gratitude.

~ ~ ~

*Kevin and Liam Marshall and
Deirdre Shalloe Marshall*

Liam, Jenny and Heather Marshall

Niamh, Jenny and Grandad

*Painting between the lines?
Liam, Heather and Grandad*

Still smiling, 2013

About the Author

Frank Marshall broadcast twenty-seven short scripts on *The Quiet Quarter* on Lyric fm and *Sunday Miscellany* and *The Living Word* on RTE Radio 1. His work was included in the 2004 and 2009 Lyric fm anthologies. A radio play, *A River Walk*, was nominated for the P.J. O'Connor Drama Awards and broadcast on RTE Radio 1 and Radio Kilkenny; in 2012 a revised version was broadcast online by Shoestring Radio Theatre on Radio KUSF, San Francisco. A stage play, *The Homecoming*, was given a public reading in the Tyrone Guthrie Centre. His poetry has appeared in *Stroan Anthology*, *Kilkenny Poetry Review*, *Reality*, *Horizons* and various journals. He has been published in *Spirituality* and *The Dubliner*. He edited the first edition of *Rhyme Rag* for the Arts Office in Kilkenny. Frank lives in Kilkenny with his wife, Maree; they have two sons and a daughter, and three grandchildren.

32149720R00099

Made in the USA
Charleston, SC
11 August 2014